# Weeds
## ON TRIAL

# Weeds ON TRIAL

## THE VERDICTS EVERY GARDENER NEEDS

### Ruth Binney

RP

RYDON
PUBLISHING

A Rydon Publishing Book
35 The Quadrant
Hassocks
West Sussex
BN6 8BP
www.rydonpublishing.co.uk
www.rydonpublishing.com

First published by Rydon Publishing in 2019
Copyright © Ruth Binney 2019

A CIP catalogue record for this book is available from the
British Library.
ISBN: 978-1-910821-27-5

Printed in Poland by BZ Graf

# CONTENTS

# Introduction

'Weeds', said AA Milne, creator of Pooh Bear and lover of the countryside 'are flowers too, once you get to know them'. Indeed they are. So even if you loathe them for being in the wrong place in your garden at the wrong time, and feel the need to remove them from your beds, it is impossible not to have some admiration for weeds. For whether they are 'wild flowers' or more cultivated garden 'thugs', weeds do have the most remarkable ability to thrive in almost any environment.

Add to this weeds' edible, medical and many other uses, and their facility for attracting bees and other pollinators to the garden, and the result is a collection of plants with fascinating lifestyles and history. When, however, you've read the detailed evidence for the defence and prosecution put forward for the annual, biennial and perennial weeds included in these pages, you may still, quite justifiably, feel that the final verdicts demand that most should be purged from your plot.

## Strategies for success

In the grand scheme of evolution, weeds have achieved their success through a whole range of strategies. They are nature's ultimate opportunists, whether thriving in any soil – or almost none – resisting the hardest of frosts, and either living for years on end or having the shortest of life cycles. Even a single weed plant can produce thousands of seeds in a single season and these can germinate quickly in low temperatures and cramped conditions – and remain dormant but viable for decades. Equally vibrant are weeds' vegetative qualities. Using stems and roots, often modified for quick spreading, they can almost literally run riot in a matter of weeks or produce corms and bulbs below ground that will stay dormant until ready to sprout and multiply with ease.

### With the animals

Like all flowering plants, weeds evolved in tandem with animals and the relationship endures today. So not only can weed seeds pass undigested through bird and animal intestines but hairy fruits can be spread about simply by clinging to feathers, fur, or the clothes and boots we wear for gardening. And evolution continues.

We probably should not be surprised that some weeds are now adding to their tick list resistance to herbicides or the microorganisms that would normally cause their decay in the soil.

In an age when the health of the world's population of bees and other pollinators is under threat – and that of many butterflies and moths – many weed species can be extremely useful, especially if allowed to thrive in a wilder part of the garden. Their blooms may be superficially less attractive than those of your 'good' garden plants but many have beautiful blooms that definitely deserve to flower. Certainly you may need to keep these weeds deadheaded, but the rewards can be huge. Equally, many weeds can still provide good food, as they have done since long before the concept of the weed existed. Foraging in your garden for leaves, fruits, seeds and shoots as our ancestors did for necessity can be hugely rewarding.

## Good health

Throughout human history, many of the plants we now call weeds have been a highly valuable source of healing. Among the most ancient, traced to a Neanderthal burial site in northern Iraq, are the grape hyacinth, a plant included here as a garden 'thug'. The oldest written record of medicinal plants is contained in the *Ebers Papyrus* of ancient Egypt compiled between 3000 and 1500 BCE. Among the species listed are mint, valued then as now for aiding digestion. And from around 1,500 years from its publication in around CE 55 *De Materia Medica*, by the ancient Greek physician Dioscorides, was the herbalists' 'bible'.

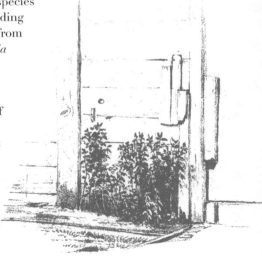

In medieval Europe, Benedictine monasteries became the main sources of herbalism. Essentially, every plant was considered to have a use, so the concept of the weed did not really exist. Women were vital in administering herbal medicines, among them Hildegard of Bingen whose medical text *Causae et Curae* dates to 1151. In the 16th and 17th centuries two key herbalists became the first to be published in English. These were John Gerard, author of *Historie of Plants* (1597) and Nicholas Culpeper, compiler of *The English Physician* – commonly known as *Culpeper's Complete Herbal* (1653). Despite their authors' lack of knowledge of human physiology, these herbals remain in print today as a springboard for continuing research into the remarkable medicinal qualities of so many weeds.

## The weeder's task

Weeding may be a chore or a pleasure, depending on the state of your body or mind – and that of your garden. The treatments suggested here will help you devise the best way of dealing with them. Certainly weeds are easiest to remove when the soil is damp and it helps to have the right tools, persistence, energy and if really necessary a weedkiller, although I would urge the ideal of being organic except in extreme circumstances. There are undoubtedly several extremely problematic weeds, some of which you are legally required to keep under control, as detailed in the book's final section.

We modern weeders may not all agree with the artist and gardener Anna Lea Merritt (1844–1930) writing in her 1908 book *The Artist's Garden* that 'a really long day of weeding is a restful experience', but may well appreciate her thoughts following a day of weeding: '… my fingers are bleeding, knees tottering, back bent, dress muddy and soaking, and shoes offensive to my tidy maid; but I have attained the most profound inward peace, and the blessed belief of having uprooted all my enemies.'

Great thanks are due to Robert Ertle and his team for putting this book together – designer Prudence Rogers, editor Verity Graves-Morris and assistant Eleanor Foot. As you study these verdicts I do hope that you'll learn to love at least some of the weeds in your garden.

Ruth Binney, Yeovil, Somerset, 2019

# Annuals
## and
# Biennials

nnual weeds – those that germinate, flower and die in the same year – and biennials, which take two years to develop and flower before they die off, essentially owe their success to the seeds they produce, sometimes in the tens of thousands. The old wives' saying 'one year's seed, seven years weed' could not be more appropriate for these weeds. Their seeds, easily spread, are not only able to germinate rapidly, even at low temperatures, but can stay dormant in the soil for decades. Add to these attributes such adaptations as frost resistance and you have weeds that are perfectly suited not only for colonizing any spare patch of ground in your garden but for travelling the world.

The seeds of annual weeds are made and released by a variety of efficient means, from the explosive fruits of the hairy bitter-cress and Himalayan balsam to the sticky 'burs' of goosegrass which travel on animal fur and gardeners' garments. Then there are the parachutes – the plumed fruits of prickly sow thistles and groundsel – and the seeds like those of fat hen and knotgrass spread via the intestines of the birds that relish them for food.

From the edible leaves of red deadnettle to the nectar filled flowers of the spear thistle on which bees and butterflies feed with relish, and whose flower heads you can cook and enjoy like artichokes, annual weeds have many other excellent qualities. Medicinally they have massive potential, as with the knotgrass, used in Chinese medicine for more than 2,000 years and now being developed as an effective cure for fungal infections.

## Quick verdicts

These are a few more of the many annual and biennial weeds that will take the opportunity to flourish in your garden in addition to those included in this section:

**Black nightshade** (*Solanum nigrum* subspecies *nigrum*) – white flowers like those of a tomato and small black poisonous fruits eaten and spread by birds.

**Gallant soldier or Kew weed** (*Galinsoga parviflora*) – escaped from Kew Gardens in the 1860s. Spreads by parachute seeds which mature in composite flower heads.

**Petty spurge** (*Euphorbia peplus*) – close relative of the cultivated euphorbias. The latex it exudes, although poisonous and an extreme irritant, is being used in cancer research.

**Annual meadow grass** (*Poa annua*) – the most common annual grass found as a garden weed. Can flower and set seed all year.

C

# CHARLOCK (OR WILD MUSTARD)

*Sinapis arvensis*

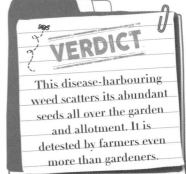

## VERDICT

This disease-harbouring weed scatters its abundant seeds all over the garden and allotment. It is detested by farmers even more than gardeners.

### FOR THE PROSECUTION

Charlock is particularly unwelcome as it is a host for the turnip fly and other vegetable pests, and for fungal diseases that attack your prized brassicas. Worse still, it can harbour club root, a condition affecting not only edible brassicas but also such ornamental relatives as wallflowers, stocks and aubretias, stunting top growth and, below ground, producing swollen, deformed often fatally inefficient roots.

## FOR THE DEFENCE

If you let charlock flourish in sunny outposts of your plot (it won't grow in the shade) its sweet nectar will be a magnet for bees and for small and large white butterflies which will also choose it as a site for egg laying. Young leaves of charlock have long been cooked and eaten. If you do choose to consume them take great care (see below).

## THE TREATMENT

Easy to pull, dig or hoe up, especially when young, but it needs to be caught – or at the very least deadheaded – before the flowers turn into ripe seeds. Or use a weedkiller of your choice.

## Secrets of success

The charlock fruit (a siliqua) is long and thin, rather like a bird's beak, and contains a pair of valves which open as the fruit dries, expelling the seeds. While each siliqua may contain between one and two dozen seeds, in a season a single plant can produce 4,000 or more, and these can stay dormant in the soil for decades.

### WARNING!

If picked from a plant that is in flower, the leaves will contain a chemical that can cause severe stomach irritation. The seeds, like those of its close relation the oilseed rape plant, also contain the same irritant.

## Did you know ?

• Charlock is native to the Mediterranean and may well have been brought to Britain by the Romans.
• Oil from charlock seeds was once pressed out and used as 'lighter fuel' for household lamps.
• In recent times, charlock appears to have evolved considerable natural resistance to a wide range of herbicides, making it even more disliked by farmers.

# CHICKWEED

*Stellaria media*

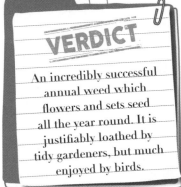

## VERDICT

An incredibly successful annual weed which flowers and sets seed all the year round. It is justifiably loathed by tidy gardeners, but much enjoyed by birds.

## FOR THE PROSECUTION

Chickweed can survive both frost and drought. In just a few months a single plant can produce 2,500 seeds, which can lie dormant in the soil for 25 years – and possibly 40 – before germinating. The slender stems straggle over the ground, forming themselves into mats as roots spring from stem nodes. And chickweed not only robs the soil of nitrogen but attracts foliage-destroying thrips, and viruses like tomato spotted wilt that can be transmitted to your crops.

## FOR THE DEFENCE

Chickweed seeds are good food for small birds – hence its common name. The edible leaves can be eaten raw, while leaves, stems and flowers can be added to soups and casseroles or mixed with other vegetables. The leaves are rich in a wide range of vitamins (including A, B and C) and minerals including potassium. The plants also have good medicinal attributes.

## THE TREATMENT

**Promptness is key. Always try to get plants out of the ground before they set seeds. Any good, thickly-spread mulch such as woodchips (see Mulching) will help to prevent germination. On bare ground, any non-selective weedkiller containing acetic or pelargonic acid will control chickweed successfully, or try one containing fatty acids. Be sure to protect nearby plants and, in the vegetable garden, wait until autumn when most crops have been harvested.**

## Remarkable qualities

The many traditional uses of chickweed include relief of everything from constipation to kidney complaints and pains:

 Chickweed ointment has long been applied to irritated skin.

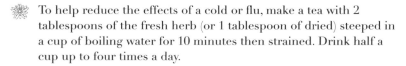 To help reduce the effects of a cold or flu, make a tea with 2 tablespoons of the fresh herb (or 1 tablespoon of dried) steeped in a cup of boiling water for 10 minutes then strained. Drink half a cup up to four times a day.

'Chickweed water' is an old wives' potion for losing weight.

Although native to Britain, chickweed has now travelled to virtually every country in the world, spread by everything from birds to boots.

# COMMON GROUNDSEL

*Senecio vulgaris*

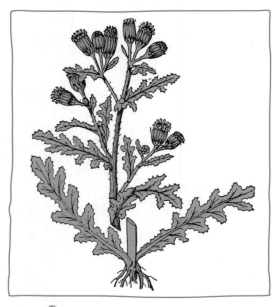

## VERDICT

A weed that can grow anywhere and everywhere but is easy to hoe out. It flowers almost all the year round and its sticky seeds are spread with ease.

### FOR THE PROSECUTION

Groundsel will survive snow and frost, thrive in the shallowest soil (and even in tiny gaps in walls) but favours recently dug or disturbed soil. Potentially one plant can create up to 1,000 offspring; its seeds are like mini dandelion parachutes that fly away in the slightest breeze. And when it rains the seeds quickly get sticky enough to cling to your boots, tools or to birds' feet.

## FOR THE DEFENCE

The seeds of groundsel are good food for sparrows and other small birds, and plants help to sustain ragwort flea beetles, gallflies, ragwort seed flies and other insects as well as the caterpillars of the cinnabar moth, flame shoulder moth and the ragwort plume moth. Rabbits can munch the leaves with no ill effects.

## WARNING!

Once a cure-all administered for everything from worm infestations in children to epilepsy, groundsel was also believed to cure 'the king's evil' (see Lesser celandine) an infection thought curable only by a royal touch. Because the leaves have been discovered to contain powerful alkaloids capable of causing severe liver infection, it is not used today.

## THE TREATMENT

Easy enough to pull out by hand, or dislodge with a hoe when young, but try to avoid letting groundsel set seeds as these can germinate in as few as five days. Another excellent reason for ridding the vegetable garden of groundsel is that it can harbour the fungus responsible for deadly black root rot in peas, beans, carrots and tomatoes – plus cucumbers and their relations.

## In the name

• Groundsel gets its name from the Anglo-Saxon *grondeswyle* meaning 'ground glutton'.
• *Senecio* comes from the Latin *senex* – 'old' – from the white hair tufts on the seed heads that look like the heads of balding men.

# FAT HEN

*Chenopodium album*

### VERDICT

A nuisance in the garden because of its copious seed production, and a trigger of hay fever, but has been eaten and enjoyed for centuries.

## FOR THE PROSECUTION

Every fat hen plant can make up to 3,000 seeds in a single lifetime, and these will germinate even a few weeks after being shed. Fat hen pollen is one of the many culprits in provoking hay fever.

## FOR THE DEFENCE

As an alternative vegetable, fat hen is worth encouraging and even cultivating in the garden, especially if you can confine it sufficiently to form a small stand rather than a series of scattered individual plants. The seeds are a favourite food of greenfinches.

## THE TREATMENT

As with all annuals, fat hen is best removed by hand before it sets seeds – and ideally before it flowers, not least because the flowers and immature fruits can be hard to distinguish except on close examination. Mulching is a most effective way of preventing germination.

## A veritable feast

Fat hen has been enjoyed, commonly mixed with grains such as barley, since the Iron Age and archaeologists have discovered it at domestic sites across Europe. Like the shepherd's purse (see Capsella bursa-pastoris) it was one of the last foods eaten by Tollund Man whose mummified remains, dating to the 4th century BCE, were discovered in Scandinavia in 1950.

The tens of thousands of black seeds produced by each plant are rich in protein, vitamin A, calcium, phosphorus and potassium. And their high fat content would have made them an excellent food to eat in cold weather or in times of famine.

### WARNING!

Although fat hen leaves are edible, they are high in oxalic acid, which is potentially harmful to the digestive system. This can be neutralized to a small degree by mixing leaves with natural yoghurt.

## Did you know?

⌀ In Africa and Asia fat hen, a cousin of the newly popular Andean high-protein grain quinoa, is cultivated as a grain and vegetable crop.

⌀ Fat hen is a closely related to the much less weedy Good King Henry (*Chenopodium*), which still grows on some medieval sites.

⌀ Other names for fat hen include Jack (or John) o'the Nile or muckweed from its love of growing near composting animal remains. Or it may be known as white goosefoot, lamb's quarters or pigweed.

# FIELD PENNYCRESS

*Thlaspi arvense*

## VERDICT

A prolific seed producer whose seeds can remain viable in the soil for more than three decades. Its fruiting heads are loved by flower arrangers.

### FOR THE PROSECUTION

From March to October the closely packed flowers of this crucifer self-pollinate to produce round, flat penny-like seed pods which ripen, dry, then forcibly eject their contents. These seeds germinate quickly to produce plants that successfully overwinter. Ironically, the more nutrient-rich loam you have in your plot the more field pennycress will thrive.

## FOR THE DEFENCE

Even the 'ordinary' plant, once fruiting, can be used in floral arrangements, and it is visited by a wide variety of insects including the cabbage white butterfly. Medicinally, field pennycress has many proven effects, notably in the treatment of rheumatism and kidney and urinary problems. It can also quell inflammation and sepsis and act as an antibiotic effective against staphylococci and streptococci.

## THE TREATMENT

**Pull, dig or hoe up small plants and compost them or dig them directly into the soil as long as they don't have seed heads. Once large they can produce hefty taproots. You may like to encourage some to thrive in a convenient location if you want them for flower arrangements.**

F

## That's surprising

- Field pennycress, often aided by genetic manipulation, is increasingly being cultivated as biofuel. Its seeds yield more than twice as much oil as soya beans.

- The cultivated variety 'Green Bells' produces seed head that are particularly good for flower arrangements.

- Ground pennycress seeds are commonly used as a mustard substitute.

- The leaves are edible (and strong tasting) when young, but are unbearably bitter once the flowers start to appear.

- The milk of cows will be tainted if these animals eat the plant.

## All in a name

Field pennycress has acquired the obvious name of stinkweed from the strong smell of the crushed leaves. Some say it is like a mixture of garlic and mustard, others describe it as foetid. Yet other names are fanweed, Frenchweed or mithridate mustard, the last of these describing a medicine believed to act as a universal antidote to both poison and disease.

# GOOSEGRASS (OR CLEAVERS)

*Galium aparine*

## VERDICT

Quick growing sticky stems of goosegrass will quickly overwhelm small plants. Its sticky fruits, which can be ground as a coffee substitute, travel far and wide.

### FOR THE PROSECUTION

In a single season a goosegrass plant can grow to 3 m (10 ft) and once established in a hedge it becomes a beast to get rid of. The fruits easily detach themselves from the parent plant and the seeds within germinate easily in both spring and autumn.

### FOR THE DEFENCE

Modern analysis has revealed that goosegrass is rich in calcium, sodium and silica and is good for the teeth and hair when taken as an infusion (with the usual safety precautions). For centuries children have had fun playing chasing games and sticking goosegrass onto each other.

## THE TREATMENT

**Easy to pull out by hand, but always wear gloves – the whole plant is covered with hooked bristles that are most painful if pressed into the skin. And wear clothes that will hamper the fruits from sticking (cleaving) to cut down the risk of spreading them around the garden. Most annual weeds can be composted – but not goosegrass – the fruits will lie dormant until put back into the soil. Take them to your local tip or burn them if you're allowed.**

## Many more uses

❋ Goosegrass is a favourite food for geese. It was once chopped up and fed to goslings.

❋ In Staffordshire it is mixed with nettles and used in beer brewing.

❋ Bundles of goosegrass stems were used to strain milk in ancient Greece, a practice that persisted in Europe up to the end of the 19th century.

❋ The dried fruits have long been used to top the pins employed in lace making.

❋ Goosegrass roots can be used to make a natural red dye.

❋ The seeds have been collected, dried and made into an ersatz coffee.

## Many names

Take your pick from this expressive selection of other common names for goosegrass from around Britain:
• Bobby buttons
• claggy meggies
• clyders
• clivvers
• gosling weed
• goose bumps
• gollenweed
• herriff
• sweethearts
• kisses
• Robin-run-the-hedge
• sticky willy
• stickleback

# HAIRY BITTER-CRESS

*Cardamine hirsuta*

## VERDICT

A peppery tasting but persistent nuisance whose seeds germinate at the same time as those of newly planted crops, making weeding very hit and miss.

## FOR THE PROSECUTION

Seeds of hairy bitter-cress get into the garden unnoticed, often in the soil of container grown plants or in compost. These then germinate easily all year round into frost hardy plants typified by rosettes of leaves that hug the ground.

## FOR THE DEFENCE

With its peppery taste, very similar to watercress, hairy bitter-cress makes a great salad ingredient, though be sure to wash it well before cooking or eating it. You can use it in a soup or as a substitute for basil in a pesto. In some regions, hairy bitter-cress acts as a winter trap for aphids; pull and compost these useful plants in spring.

## THE TREATMENT

Simple to ease or dig out but it can come back remarkably quickly, although it is possible to suppress it successfully with a mulch of bark or compost. But be very careful when hoeing or hand weeding it from amongst newly established vegetables crops such as parsnips and beetroot. On paths you may need a weed killer, but an organic type (see Weedkillers and how to use them) is likely to be successful.

## Explosive secrets

Hairy bitter-cress is one of the most efficient examples of weeds with explosive fruits. A large plant can produce as many as 50,000 seeds in its lifetime, contained in groups of 14 to 30 inside pods divided into two by papery valves. As the pods mature, these dry out and stretch so that when the pod is touched they instantaneously curl up, thrusting the seeds into the air.

Experiments have proved that even in still air seeds are able to travel as much as 80 cm (32 in), and a fair number 60 cm (2 ft). They may germinate where they land or be transported on boots, tools and on the feet of birds and other animals.

## Very similar

Slightly taller and equally weedy is the wavy or wood bitter-cress, *Cardamine flexuosa*. This can be biennial and perennial as well as annual and favours mostly wet and poorly drained soil. Its flowers are attractive to hoverflies, flea beetles and to orange tip and green-veined white butterflies.

# HEDGE MUSTARD (OR BARBED WIRE PLANT)

*Sisymbrium officinale*
*(formerly Erysimum) officinale*

**VERDICT**

A favourite food for cabbage white caterpillars, this frost-hardy, prolific all-year seed producer makes substantial tap roots, especially in its second year of growth.

**FOR THE PROSECUTION**

This biennial or sometimes annual crucifer with small yellow flowers looks like a straggly version of oilseed rape. One of Britain's most common plants, its black seeds, numbering more than 9,000 on a large plant in a single season, germinate most rapidly in disturbed ground. Seeds ejected from its elongated pods (siliquae) germinate in autumn into small rosettes which then overwinter with ease.

## FOR THE DEFENCE

Long valued for its flavour and medicinal qualities, hedge mustard is a draw for cabbage white butterflies whose eggs hatch into myriad caterpillars on the plants, (but not necessarily in preference to your brassica crops). Use young, mustardy-tasting leaves in salads or omelettes or add them to a soup or green sauce. If you have the patience, collect and crush the seeds for a condiment.

## THE TREATMENT

**Pull, dig or hoe up plants, ideally before they flower – usually from May to October – and set seed, although for large patches you might need to resort to a weedkiller. If your garden or allotment adjoins arable land you will be doing the farmer a huge favour by stopping it from spreading. Plants without seed heads can be composted or dug straight back into the soil as a green manure, but heat treat seeded plants before composting (see Composting weeds).**

## For the voice

In the 16th century, following the claim by the Frenchman Guillaume Rondelet of Montpelier that he endowed a choirboy with 'the voice of an angel' by giving him hedge mustard, it was nicknamed the 'singer's plant'. It was also favoured as a gargle and medicinal voice improver by French actors and politicians.

## Medicinal qualities

Both fresh and dried hedge mustard leaves and flowers are included in herbal infusions for loosening and dissolving mucus in the mouth and throat, soothing sore throats and treating bronchitis. Their key ingredients are sulfur compounds. It is also effective in stimulating gastric juices and treating digestive problems such as bloating and indigestion. In Tibet it is used to ease food poisoning symptoms.

# HERB ROBERT (OR STINKING BOB)

*Geranium robertianum*

## VERDICT

So attractive that it is almost good enough to keep in the garden despite its acrid smell. Effective in deterring pests and attracting insects.

## FOR THE PROSECUTION

What makes herb Robert so successful is its highly efficient seed-scattering mechanism. Not only can the long, thin seed capsules, which look like birds' bills, shoot their contents 6 m (20 ft) or more, but the seeds are covered with sticky fibres which adhere easily to clothes, shoes, animal fur and tools. It's a particular nuisance when it germinates among vegetable and salad seedlings.

## FOR THE DEFENCE

Pretty pink flowers sit atop herb Robert's red stems and its delicate fern like leaves, which turn brilliant red in autumn, can deter mosquitoes from biting if rubbed onto the skin. If you put some leaves in your cat or dog's bed it will help deter fleas. It is attractive to bees, the barred carpet moth and long-tongued hoverflies, but helpfully distasteful to rabbits and deer.

## THE TREATMENT

**Short, shallow branching roots make herb Robert very easy to pull out by hand, but take good care not to disturb nearby plants. Where you have plants prone to insect attack, such as tomatoes or brassicas, leave as many growing as you can, but nip off deadheads to prevent them from setting seed.**

## Healing powers

According to ancient medical practice known as the doctrine of signatures, the healing abilities of plants were ascribed by their looks. So herb Robert, from its redness, was judged to be effective for blood and bleeding problems. Ulcers and gingivitis are other conditions traditionally treated with herb Robert.

Modern analysis has found that herb Robert has antiseptic qualities and can act as an antioxidant able to boost immune system activity. It also contains tannins and essential oils.

## How named?

• The name may be a corruption of the Latin *ruber*, meaning red, or could refer to the 11th century French saint Abbot Robert of Molerne.
• Other common names include bachelor's buttons, Jenny wren, Robin redshanks, red breast, dragon's blood and red bobby's eye.

# HIMALAYAN (OR INDIAN) BALSAM

*Impatiens glandulifera*

**VERDICT**

Be aware! It is illegal to plant or otherwise cause this pretty weed to grow in the wild in the UK. This dangerously invasive weed is a potential menace if it gets into your garden.

## FOR THE PROSECUTION

Rapidly germinating water-resistant seeds that explode from the merest touch on ripe seed pods, plus stems from which new roots will spring from any node near the ground, allow Himalayan balsam to spread extremely quickly. And because it can tolerate considerable shade it smothers everything in its immediate environment, destroying valuable habitats in the process.

## FOR THE DEFENCE

There is little to recommend this weed, and although it is attractive to bees, they are likely to visit Himalayan balsam flowers in preference to those of native species and vital food crops. Young leaves, shoots and seed pods are edible and the flowers can be made into a jam.

## THE TREATMENT

**Keep a watchful eye for new plants and pull or dig them out immediately. This isn't difficult, especially for small stands, as the roots are shallow. Do all you can to prevent them from flowering and setting seed.**

**A weedkiller is likely to be most effective (see Weedkillers and how to use them), whether a non-selective contact type, best sprayed on before plants flower, or a glyphosate weedkiller at any stage. Glyphosate will have maximum effect when plants are growing most vigorously, usually in May or June, but an autumn application is advisable. Take great care with plants growing in water as weedkiller can have adverse effects on 'good' plants.**

**As long as they've dried out completely, pulled plants that haven't flowered can be composted. If in doubt, put plant remains into a separate bag, take it to your local disposal site and declare the contents.**

## That's amazing

• Seeds can shoot up to 7 m (22 ft) from the parent plants.
• The plant first arrived in British gardens in 1839, admired for its handsome stance and pretty pink helmet-shaped flowers.
• Because of its seeds pods, Himalayan balsam is also known as jumping jack or touch-me-not.
• Experiments with rust fungus are showing promising signs for eradicating this weed.

# KNOTGRASS (OR IRONWEED)

*Polygonum aviculare*

## VERDICT

This tasty vegetable can thrive in any soil. Although notorious for its seeds, which can survive in the ground for many years and germinate quickly, these are good food for birds.

### FOR THE PROSECUTION

This spreading annual particularly favours a dry, sandy environment. Knotgrass, immediately identifiable from its wiry rather straggly and spreading stems, with distinctive knots where the leaves and stem join, can grow a large tap root up to 1 m (3 ft) long, which penetrates the soil in just a few weeks. The many seeds are produced from the small pink or white flowers blooming from midsummer.

## FOR THE DEFENCE

Knotgrass leaves and young stems make a tasty vegetable, either raw or cooked. They are rich in calcium, zinc, phosphorus and carotine. Small birds of many kinds relish knotgrass seeds, a liking reflected in the species name *aviculare*, from the Latin *avicula* meaning little bird. The plant also has a range of medicinal qualities.

## THE TREATMENT

**Pull out by hand when small, or hoe or dig out if larger, and always wear gloves as the sap can irritate the skin. Use a weeding knife to remove it from paths, patios and walls. For lawn invaders, push as many of the shoots upwards as you can before mowing. This will weaken plants, which should die off at the end of the season. As a deterrent, mulching works well, or use a fast-acting weedkiller (see Dealing with weeds).**

## Medicinal attributes

✚ Crushed leaves have been used to staunch nosebleeds – a so-called styptic effect. The same property makes it useful for treating wounds.

✚ Its diuretic qualities make knotgrass suitable for helping to improve kidney function. It may also help to treat kidney stones.

✚ Knotgrass has been used in Chinese medicine for over 2,000 years. Modern analysis has proved its effectiveness in treating fungal infections and endorsed its styptic qualities.

## Family evils

Knotgrass is a close relation of the feared Japanese knotweed (see *Fallopia japonica*). Both belong to the botanical family Polygonaceae, as does the rampant garden climber the Russian vine (see Russian vine, or Mile-a-minute).

# PRICKLY (OR SPINY) SOW THISTLE

*Sonchus asper*

## VERDICT

From yellow flowers highly attractive to pollinators come vast numbers of seeds which can then germinate into seedlings at almost any time of year.

### FOR THE PROSECUTION

This sow thistle spreads its copious seed-containing fruits by means of fluffy airborne 'plumes'. A single plant can release as many as 60,000 in a single season. If left to grow to their fullest extent, plants will put down creeping rootstocks, especially on recently cultivated soil and near walls. Seedlings often overwinter making plants biennial as well as annual.

### FOR THE DEFENCE

The yellow dandelion-like flowers, which bloom from June to October, are attractive to bees, hoverflies and other insect pollinators. The young leaves, with less well defined 'teeth' than the mature ones, are edible and remarkably succulent. Sow thistles also act as 'reservoirs' for aphids, keeping them off your crops and flowers.

## THE TREATMENT

Hand weed sow thistles as soon as you see them and do your best to prevent them from setting seed. You may need to take a spade or large fork to any that have grown tall – just cutting them down to ground level will merely stimulate them to produce new top growth. Always wear gloves as a precaution against its spines and the latex that exudes from cut stems. If not seeded, plants can be composted or dug straight back into the ground. Large expanses of sow thistles may respond best to a weedkiller, preferably organic.

## That's amazing

- The milk yield of farmyard sows feeding their young was once believed to be increased if the animals ate prickly sow thistle.

- Drinking the milky latex from prickly sow thistles was once thought to be a help to nursing human mothers.

- Prickly sow thistle seeds can pass unchanged (and still able to germinate) through the digestive systems of earthworms, birds and even cattle.

## Medicinal matters

Scientific studies with extracts of prickly sow thistle have shown it to be effective in killing harmful bacteria including *E. coli* and some pathogenic fungi such as *Candida albicans*. This makes it a promising treatment for boils, wounds and fungal skin conditions. It is also showing potential for treating liver and kidney diseases and disorders.

# RED (OR PURPLE) DEADNETTLE

*Lamium purpureum*

## VERDICT

A vigorous clump former with attractively coloured leaves and flowers, loved by bees. Needs virtually year-round attention. Can make a good green manure.

## FOR THE PROSECUTION

The seeds of the red deadnettle, produced from flowers that bloom from February right through to November or December, fall and germinate readily close to the parent plant which means that it is a constant concern for the tidy gardener. Once its seeds are in your ground this weed is almost impossible to get rid of completely.

## FOR THE DEFENCE

The maroon-tinged leaves of this deadnettle, although they look like those of the 'regular' nettle, have no sting so are safe to handle without gloves. Its maroon nectar-filled flowers are attractive to bees, and the leaves are both edible and medicinal, so plants definitely deserve a place in a wilder, sunny spot in your garden or allotment.

## THE TREATMENT

**Pull or dig out young plants, or hoe when small enough, before the seeds (known as nutlets) form and disperse, and add them to the compost heap. Or dig plants back into the soil immediately as a green manure.**

## Good to eat

Young leaves of this deadnettle can be eaten raw in salads or cooked and eaten as a tasty green vegetable. Use with or instead of spinach or watercress in a hot or cold soup, with cream added if you wish. Traditionally they were used as feed for the pigs that were kept by cottagers to provide meat for country families throughout the year.

## Medicinal qualities

The red deadnettle was once called into use to treat the 'king's evil' or scrofula, a type of tuberculosis that affects body parts outside the lungs, notably the lymph nodes in the neck, and which can also result in unsightly skin eruptions. Crushed, fresh leaves can stem bleeding from cuts and wounds and are added to poultices intended to stem prolonged haemorrhaging. It may also be suitable for treating problems of the kidneys and the digestive tract.

## Benign relation

The henbit deadnettle (*Lamium amplexicale*), also an annual but with round-edged leaves and slimmer, paler flowers, is much less invasive and worth keeping in the garden in small quantities to attract bees.

**See also** White deadnettle (*Lamium album*).

# SCARLET PIMERNEL

*Anagallis arvensis*

**VERDICT**

Never seriously invasive,
and rightly loved for its
pretty red (but sometimes
pink, purple or lilac)
flowers. Deserves to
survive in most places
in the garden.

## FOR THE PROSECUTION

From flowers that appear in quick
succession from May or June until
November – or the first hard frost
– the scarlet pimpernel reproduces
most efficiently by seed, each plant
shedding as many as 1,000 and more
in a single year. It can be a nuisance
when it germinates between
vegetable seedling and in mild
winters, plants will often survive to
flower for a second season.

## FOR THE DEFENCE

A delight to have in the garden in
most circumstances. Not for nothing
is this pretty, bright red flower known
as the poor man's weatherglass,
change-of-the-weather, shepherd's
sundial and weather flower. It will
invariably close its petals if the sky
becomes overcast ahead of rain, and
its leaves are useful as an instant
garden remedy to relieve the pain of
insect bites and stings.

## THE TREATMENT

**Simply pull plants out by hand, or use a trowel, hand fork or hoe. Avoid all but organic weedkillers.**

## The flower forecaster

Although it can predict rain the scarlet pimpernel will close its petals by 2.00 pm, whatever the weather, and keep them shut until 8.00 am. If the petals open fully in the morning a fine day can be expected. But the reverse is not true. When the flowers fail to open first thing it is likely to remain cloudy, but the chance of rainfall is little better than about 15 per cent.

## A special name

For her 1905 novel *The Scarlet Pimpernel*, Baroness Orczy (1865–1947) chose the title from the symbol by which her enigmatic hero Sir Percy Blakeney is known. Only the band of gentlemen who assist him have knowledge of his real identity. The genus name *Anagallis* comes from the Greek *anagallo* meaning to decorate, and refers to the many flowers produced over the season.

## From times past

Since the time of ancient physicians such as Dioscorides (CE 40–90) scarlet pimpernel had an excellent reputation for treating mental illness, epilepsy, rabies and tuberculosis, as well as gallstones, cirrhosis and urinary tract infections. It was also used by herbalists to help to loosen and remove mucus from the chest and throat. Scientific studies have revealed that the plant contains highly toxic substances, so is no longer recommended for internal use.

# SHEPHERD'S PURSE

*Capsella bursa-pastoris*

## VERDICT

Its super-efficient seed producing ability, and flowers that bloom all year round, has made the shepherd's purse one of the world's most widespread weeds, but also a universal bird food.

### FOR THE PROSECUTION

In just 12 months a single shepherd's purse plant can produce 4,000 seeds or more. These germinate quickly with new plants then producing new seeds in a mere six weeks.

### FOR THE DEFENCE

The many seeds, released from distinctive heart-shaped pods, are good food for chaffinches and other garden birds.

## THE TREATMENT

Very easy to pull out by hand or with the assistance of a hand fork or trowel when young, but mature plants may need deeper digging. A serious infestation might call for a weedkiller, but only as a last resort. Ideally, remove plants before they have a chance to set seed; look carefully for the flowers which are formed and mature from the base of the flower stalk.

## What's in a name?

The shepherd's purse is named scientifically from the Latin *capsula*, meaning 'little box' and from *bursa*, a purse, and *pastor*, a shepherd. That's because the shape of the seed pods resembles the leather bags that shepherds once slung onto their belts to take food out into the field. In addition, the seeds that tumble from the ripe fruit are like coins being shaken out of a purse.

Other common names, including pickpocket and mother's heart, come from the old childhood game of asking someone to pick and open a seed capsule, then accusing them of breaking their mother's heart.

## An ancient history

Seeds of shepherd's purse were found in the stomach of the Tollund Man, who was buried in a bog in what is present-day Denmark in around 400–300 BCE. This chimes with the belief that shepherd's purse has been eaten as a peppery-tasting vegetable for hundreds of years. In Japan it is still an essential ingredient of Nanakusa-Gayu or seven-herb soup, traditionally served each year on 7 January.

Traditional medicinal uses of shepherd's purse include treatment for bleeding (both internal and external), urinary infections, reducing hemorrhoids and for reducing menstrual bleeding. During World War I soldiers picked and used it to help stop blood flow from their wounds.

# SMOOTH SOW THISTLE (OR MILK THISTLE)

*Sonchus oleraceus*

**VERDICT**

Quickly makes a long tap root and can often overwinter. Has edible leaves and makes many fruits whose seeds germinate readily in cultivated soil.

## FOR THE PROSECUTION

Smooth sow thistles spread their copious seed-containing fruits by means of fluffy airborne 'plumes', formed in just a week from when the flowers first open. A single plant can make between 5,000 and a massive 40,000 seeds. It should not be confused with the purple flowered medicinal *Silybum marianum*.

## FOR THE DEFENCE

The yellow dandelion-like flowers, borne from June to August, or earlier in southern Britain, are attractive to both bees and hoverflies. The young leaves are edible and can be eaten in salads or cooked like spinach and have medicinal qualities.

## THE TREATMENT

**Dig out these thistles as soon as you see them and do your best to prevent them from setting seed. You may need to take a spade or large fork to any that have grown tall. Always wear gloves as a precaution against the milky sap exuded by the plant's cut surfaces. Large expanses of sow thistles may respond best to a weedkiller, preferably organic.**

## Myth, folklore and medicine

According to the Roman naturalist Pliny the Elder, the Greek hero Theseus became endowed with strength to slay the Minotaur by eating a dish of smooth sow thistle.

Children in Wiltshire have traditionally played the game 'silver and gold' in which a smooth sow thistle head is slit open. Any lucky enough to find those with riper yellow seeds inside – the gold – were declared to be winners.

Medicinally, smooth sow thistle leaves have been added to poultices to relieve swellings and the plant's latex used to treat warts.

Smooth sow thistle leaves are thought to strengthen and revive the creatures that eat them – notably rabbits and hares. Male hares are said to increase in strength by eating it when they 'go mad' in the spring.

## Naming matters

The name *Sonchus* comes from the Greek word for hollow and relates to the nature of the plants' stems. The smooth sow thistle has many telling alternative names including rabbit's meat, rabbit's victuals, swine thistle, dog's thistle, hare's colwort and hare's lettuce.

**See also** Prickly sow thistle (*Sonchus asper*).

# SPEAR (OR SCOTCH) THISTLE

*Cirsium vulgare*

A prodigious seed producer and robust annual or biennial whose nectar-rich flowers are a magnet for pollinators. You are legally obliged to prevent it from spreading to neighbouring land.

## FOR THE PROSECUTION

Spear thistles must be controlled because they compete with and smother arable crops and harbour harmful insect pests. Their spines can also lodge in sheep fleeces, hampering shearing. A small plant quickly forms a hard-to-remove tap root, especially on recently disturbed soil. Each plant produces around 4,000 feathered, airborne seeds per summer; these germinate readily in the autumn, overwintering well.

## Scots or not?

There is much debate over whether or not the spear thistle was the type chosen by the kings of Scotland for their emblem. Although it rarely grows wild north of the Border, some scholars favour the cotton thistle (*Onopordum acanthium*) largely from its similarity to the thistles common in Scots heraldry. The spear thistle, by contrast, is abundant all over Scotland and its heads match closely the depictions on early coins minted by Scottish kings.

## To cook thistles

Choose the biggest heads, cut them off, then boil in salted water for about five minutes. Cool a little before peeling away the leaf-like bracts surrounding the base of each flower head. Then remove the hairy growth on top of the flat choke and serve as you would a globe artichoke warm with a vinaigrette dressing.

# Perennials

**P**ersistence, persistence, persistence. That's what it takes to be a successful perennial weed – and weeder – and it is surely no accident that many of the gardener's most dreaded weeds, including the Japanese knotweed, horsetail and ground elder, are all perennials. The weeds included here have everything it takes to establish themselves in your garden and stay there until you remove them. They do this by vegetative means and, as with dandelions and the broad-leaved dock, by creating huge numbers of easily spread fruits and seeds.

In this group of perennial weeds you'll discover in detail the wide spectrum of long-term reproductive strategies, from the bramble that sends out arching shoots called stolons that quickly root as soon as they touch the ground, to the rhizomes of the enchanter's nightshade and the stinging nettle. You'll also marvel at the aptly named runners of the slender speedwell and creeping buttercup and the strangling, twining stems of the bindweeds.

Troublesome as these weeds might seem there is much to recommend. Even the infamous Japanese knotweed will attract bees and has leaves that are edible when young. Buttercups and dandelions are magnets for bees and creeping thistles can be seen surrounded by clouds of butterflies. Many perennial weeds, including dandelions, docks and nettles are edible and many more have valuable medicinal qualities that continue to be studied and developed today.

## Quick verdicts

Other perennial weeds in addition to those described in detail in this section include:

**Green alkanet** (*Pentaglottis sempervirens*) – covered with stiff hairs. Deep purple flowers attractive to bees and hover flies. Spreads by seed.

**Procumbent yellow sorrel** (*Oxalis corniculata*) – short-lived perennial with explosive seed pods. Bright yellow flowers and edible reddish-brown leaves.

**Ground ivy** (*Glechoma hederacea*) – spreads with long stolons. Heart-shaped leaves and pale purple flowers that attract bees and long-tongued hover flies.

**Helxine** or mind-your-own-business (*Soleirolia soleirolii*) – low and fast growing with small leaves and pinkish stems. Favours damp places and lawns.

**Tree seedlings** – especially those of ash (*Fraxinus excelsior*), sycamore (*Acer pseudoplatanus*) and oak (*Quercus robur*). Dig out before they root firmly or transplant seedlings to pots or selected garden spaces to grow naturally where you want them.

B

# BRAMBLE (OR BLACKBERRY)

*Rubus fruticosus*

**VERDICT**

Fine in an informal place where they can fruit freely and accessibly. Where unwanted, brambles are almost impossible to get rid of once established.

## FOR THE PROSECUTION

Blackberries spread quickly. Each thorny, arching, woody shoot (stolon), which can rapidly reach 2.5 m (8 ft), will send out roots anywhere it touches the ground. And these roots can rapidly penetrate to around 1.5 m (4½ ft). New plants germinate easily from seeds contained in the fleshy fruits, spread by the birds and small mammals that enjoy eating the sweet, juicy berries as much as we do and eject the seeds undigested from their intestines.

## FOR THE DEFENCE

Tasty blackberries freeze brilliantly and beyond mixing with apple have a wide culinary repertoire. Rich in vitamins, especially vitamin C, they are high in magnesium, low calorie and an excellent source of both soluble and insoluble fibre. They have proved good for the eyesight and contain anthocyanins, chemicals thought to help strengthen the immune system. The flowers are a magnet for bees, wasps, flies and small beetles of the family Syrphidae. Among the moths they attract is the marsh marigold moth.

## THE TREATMENT

**Wear thornproof gloves to remove even the youngest plants by hand. Older plants need more drastic measures and, however thorough, may leave you with small pieces of root that can easily sprout back into life. For bigger plants, cut off the top growth (a strimmer is ideal for this) and dig out the roots as well as you can. Or cut back to about 30 cm (1 ft) and apply a maximum strength glyphosate weedkiller at any time from spring to autumn. Avoid rotovating, which will spread small pieces of viable root far and wide and mulch to help prevent seed germination.**

## That's extraordinary

- Archaeological studies reveal that blackberries have been enjoyed in Britain for at least 10,000 years (since Neolithic times).

- Botanists have identified more than 2,000 individual varieties or microspecies of blackberry in Europe alone.

- A single 'bush' can produce up to 150,000 seeds in a single year.

- The female shield bug uses blackberry plants to shelter her 30–40 young.

- Orange, green and purple dyes can be made from the roots, leaves and fruit.

- It's said that blackberries shouldn't be picked and eaten after Michaelmas, 29 September, when the Devil spits on them.

# BROAD-LEAVED DOCK

*Rumex obtusifolius*

**A pernicious weed whose spread is restricted by law. Has a persistent root and thousands of easily spread fruits. The long-lasting seeds contain a chemical that prevents them from being broken down by microorganisms.**

## FOR THE PROSECUTION

The tap root of this dock, which can grow to 1.5 m (5 ft) long, is hard to remove, and the prodigious winged and water-borne fruits are endowed with sharp teeth which cling to fur and feathers of animals, and to gardeners' clothes. A single plant can produce up to 60,000 seeds a year. You are required by law to keep this weed from spreading beyond your land (see Weeds and the law).

## FOR THE DEFENCE

Like those of the curled dock (see Rumex crispus), these leaves are edible (but highly acidic) and were once used in the dairy to wrap cheese and butter, hence its alternative name of butter dock. The foliage has also been used as pig food over the centuries and are devoured by deer, though these creatures will also eat your roses and other precious plants! Natural dyes can be made from its leaves, roots and stems.

## THE TREATMENT

**Digging plants out when young is the best solution, but beyond a certain size only a weedkiller will do the job of eradication. If you choose to use a weedkiller, whether selective or 'general', apply it with great care to prevent damage to adjacent plants. Always dispose of dock roots and seeds carefully, preferably at your local tip rather than on your compost heap, and declare the contents of your bag.**

## A better-behaved relation

The common sorrel (*Rumex acetosa*) can easily take hold in a neglected lawn or in a meadow, but is far less invasive than its relatives the docks. Its leaves, although acid (like those of docks they contain oxalic acid), are pleasant to eat when made into a soup or sauce, making it a candidate for the vegetable or herb garden rather than the compost heap or tip. It makes a particularly good partner for eggs and fish.

The sorrel's acidity and edibility is reflected in its many alternative names, which include:

- sour docks
- sour dots
- sour ducks
- sour grabs
- sour sabs
- sour sap
- sour sops
- soorocks
- vinegar plant
- vinegar leaves
- green sauce
- bread and sauce

# COUCH GRASS (OR TWITCH)

C

*Elymus repens*

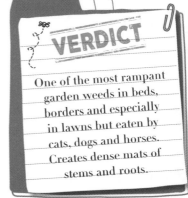

**VERDICT**

One of the most rampant garden weeds in beds, borders and especially in lawns but eaten by cats, dogs and horses. Creates dense mats of stems and roots.

## FOR THE PROSECUTION

This coarse grass, whose prominently jointed stems can grow up to 1 m (3 ft) high, produce long, thin flower stalks typical of the grass family. Its main means of reproduction is by wiry, pointed underground stems (rhizomes) which, as long as they contain just a single joint, can develop into a new plant, a capacity that makes them doggedly persistent in the garden.

52    Perennials

## FOR THE DEFENCE

Although couch grass produces seeds these are rarely fertile. Cats with furballs will choose to chew couch to make them vomit. Dogs will exhibit similar behavior too, hence the name of dog grass. Nutritionally it is rich in potassium and magnesium and the roots, if dug up, are good winter food for horses. Medicinally it has a variety of uses.

## THE TREATMENT

Digging out young plants is relatively easy – and best done – in spring and autumn. When couch invades borders a successful strategy is to dig up 'good' plants, carefully tease away all the couch rhizomes, then replace them, complete with a few handfuls of compost. This is best done when the soil is damp. In the end you may need to use glyphosate-based selective weedkiller, ideally sprayed on when shoots are young and have only four or five new leaves, but of course this won't work on a lawn (see Dealing with weeds). Wear gloves, the leaves can cut your hands.

## Named in verse

The famous author and gardener Vita Sackville-West (1892–1962) included couch grass in her 1946 poem 'The Garden':

*The couch-grass throwing roots at every node,*
*With wicked nick-names like its wicked self,*
*Twitch, quitch, quack, scutch.*

The word twitch derives from *cwice*, the name the Anglo-Saxons gave to the grass. Other common names include quackgrass and quicks, scotch and squitch.

## Saving graces

- Made into a tonic the grass acts as a mild diuretic and has been used to help prevent the formation of kidney stones. It may also help to relieve constipation and high blood pressure.

- In wartime couch grass rhizomes were used to make a kind of coffee and ground up to make a substitute for flour.

# CREEPING BUTTERCUP

*Ranunculus repens*

## VERDICT

An incredibly efficient, frost-resistant spreader with pretty, bright yellow flowers attractive to pollinators. A hard to eradicate menace on well-kept lawns.

### FOR THE PROSECUTION

Creeping buttercups spread with long runners from which new plants can grow, and has strong, deep roots that cling tenaciously to the soil making them hard to remove, especially on lawns where the leaves lie flat (see Lawns). And it can quickly regrow from even the smallest pieces of runner. It thrives best in wet, clay-rich soils.

### FOR THE DEFENCE

In the right place in the garden, such as a wildflower meadow well away from the lawn, beds and borders, you may welcome this buttercup's sunny bright yellow blooms in spring, and pollinating insects, including bees, certainly love buttercup flowers.

## THE TREATMENT

In beds and borders good weeding, followed by regular hoeing, will kill or weaken plants, but this needs to be done all through the growing season. If necessary, use a glyphosate weedkiller (see Weedkillers and how to use them), which means protecting nearby plants. For safety wear gloves; the plants contain a sap that can irritate the skin.

If your flower, fruit or vegetable beds are overwhelmed with creeping buttercups it may be best to clear the area, carefully lifting 'good' plants beforehand, then digging thoroughly, after which they can be replaced. If there is nothing worth saving, try covering the area with black plastic sheeting and leave it in place for an entire summer. Improving clay soil and lowering its acidity can also work wonders in preventing creeping buttercup growth.

## How clever

❀ In days when butter was a treat, children would put buttercup flowers under each others' chins to see the golden reflection and ask 'Do you like butter?' The answer was invariable a 'yes'. So how does this work?

❀ Buttercups have a unique method of warming their flowers to attract pollinators. Inside each petal special cells create twin layers of air which, when hit by light rays, deflects them sideways and at the same time concentrates the heat within the bloom.

❀ Visiting insects prefer warmer flowers because these help them to maintain their own body temperatures.

❀ The petals reflect light in the UV part of the spectrum, to which insect eyes are most sensitive.

C

# CREEPING THISTLE

*Cirsium arvense*

**VERDICT**

A problematic viciously prickly weed which can grow from minute pieces of root, but which attracts many butterflies. You must, by law, prevent it spreading beyond your property.

## FOR THE PROSECUTION

The thick, tough, creeping side roots of this weed, which quickly smother smaller plants struggling to grow nearby, arise from a central taproot. On these side roots (which are extremely brittle) buds are formed from which new shoots arise. This means that as pieces break off they can rapidly generate into new plants. Although the many feathered seeds are carried away in the breeze, they don't germinate very readily (see Weeds and the law).

## FOR THE DEFENCE

The honeyed perfume of creeping thistle nectar attracts clouds of butterflies, among them the painted lady, white letter hairstreak, peacock and meadow brown. Bees, too, come to feed here while the seeds are a prime attraction for goldfinches, siskin, linnets, twite and redpolls. In winter the stems create valuable overwintering sites for various insects. The roots are edible.

## THE TREATMENT

**Always wear thick gloves when dealing with these prickly monsters. Because of the way the roots break up, digging is not really a practical solution, but if you do remove them they should be bagged up, taken to your local tip and declared. If you want to garden organically, cut them down repeatedly just before flowering so that they gradually weaken. Otherwise, try a systemic weedkiller containing glyphosate and spray the foliage very thoroughly. If the leaves don't start yellowing after a week, re-apply.**

## That's a surprise

🌿 The creeping thistle has edible roots, although these can often cause flatulence.

🌿 On the Isle of Islay, the Bruichladdich distillery lists creeping thistle as an ingredient in its local gin, The Botanist.

🌿 The seeds germinate most readily when daytime temperatures reach 20 to 30°C (68 to 86°F), or when temperatures fluctuate most, as in spring and autumn.

🌿 The Canada thistle gall fly (which is fact native to Europe) lays its eggs near the stem tops, producing a swelling from which larvae emerge. Scientists are working to see if this could lead to a means of biological control.

# CURLED DOCK

*Rumex crispus*

A weed so robust and prolific that it is subject to legal restrictions and should be eliminated from the garden, despite its edibility. Even its traditional facility for cooling nettle stings is unproven.

## FOR THE PROSECUTION

Curled dock can be annual and biennial as well as perennial, but will always produce a sturdy, hard to remove tap root and can regenerate if only the root tip, which can be 1.5 m (5 ft) below the soil surface, is left in the ground. It produces fewer seeds than the broad-leaved dock (see *Rumex obtusifolius*) – usually up to 4,000 per plant – but these are easily spread by wind or water, and will remain dormant, but viable, for up to 50 years. It is covered in Britain by the Weeds Act of 1959 (see Weeds and the law).

## FOR THE DEFENCE

The leaves, once extensively used as a treatment for burns and blisters, will temporarily quell the pain of nettle stings, but only because they are cool. They certainly work best if crushed before being applied. They are also edible, although extremely acidic, so must be consumed with caution.

## THE TREATMENT

Digging plants out when young is the best solution, but beyond a certain size only weedkiller will do the job. On lawns, first cut off the flowering heads in mid to late summer before treating. Strong-growing plants can be killed individually with glyphosate but again you will need to shield all nearby plants. You'll almost certainly need to make more than one treatment. Always dispose of dock roots and seeds carefully, ideally at your local tip, declaring the contents of your load.

## Remedies and reminders

Young dock leaves are edible but the oxalic acid they contain is harmful if consumed in quantity by humans or animals and can trigger flare ups of rheumatism, kidney stones or gout. In the USA they are traditionally doused lightly with vinegar then fried with ham or bacon.

Over the years dock leaves have been applied to blisters, burns and scalds. Even more effective is to rub the cut end of a root directly onto the skin. Culpeper prescribed dock root boiled in vinegar for alleviating a range of skin conditions, and even recommended a preparation of leaves and roots for getting rid of freckles.

**See also** Broad-leaved dock (*Rumex obtusifolius*).

# DAISY

*Bellis perennis*

## VERDICT

Unwelcome on a pristine lawn, but these harbingers of spring are pretty enough to be allowed to thrive in most places in the garden.

## FOR THE PROSECUTION

In mild winters daisies will flower virtually all year and greatly strengthen their survival chances on lawns by creating leaf rosettes that lie flat to the ground. Once established they send out short horizonal shoots from which new plants arise, leading to extensive daisy patches. They can also reproduce reasonably efficiently by seed.

## FOR THE DEFENCE

Apart from its good looks, alternate picking of daisy petals chanting 'he loves me, he loves me not', until just one is left, is a long practised form of mild relaxation therapy. Equally, making daisy chains is a much-loved childhood pastime. Since ancient times young girls have adorned their heads with daisy chain 'tiaras'.

## THE TREATMENT

**Daisies are best removed by hand with a handfork or similar tool, ideally in spring and again in the autumn to prevent already vigorous plants maintaining their strength – from literally 'digging in' – over the winter months (see Lawns).**

## In times past

Although no longer part of the herbalist's armoury, daisies once had a variety of uses in medicine. John Gerard recommended sniffing the juice of the roots and leaves up the nostrils to 'purge' the head, while Culpeper advocated the use of a daisy ointment for treating wounds and inflammations. Daisy juice, he said, would also help runny eyes.

## Names and sayings

❀ The daisy's common name comes from 'day's eye', because it opens at dawn to reveal a flower with a miniature sun at its centre and closes its pink-tinged petals at sunset.

❀ The generic name *Bellis* comes from the Latin for beautiful – its specific epithet *perennis* refers to its sustained lifespan. In French it is the *marguerite* or 'pearl' and in German is *Massleib* meaning 'love measures' and also *Tausendschönen* or 'a thousand beauties'.

❀ In country places the daisy is still called bairnwort (the children's flower), mother of thousands, silver penny, bachelor's buttons and hens and chickens.

❀ In cricket a 'daisy cutter' is a very low ball that reaches the batter without bouncing.

❀ It's said that when you can tread on nine daisies at once, spring has come.

# DANDELION

*Taraxacum officinale*

## VERDICT

A persistently troublesome weed in all parts of the garden, but great for attracting bees and has edible leaves into the bargain.

## FOR THE PROSECUTION

Dandelions take hold in the garden when they send their strong tap roots, (complete with side shoots) deep into your lawn, or spring from the tightest gaps in walls and paving. Flowers can appear virtually all the year round, maturing into 'dandelion clocks', complete with parachutes, which are the plant's perfect means of seed spreading. These parachutes are known to travel as much as 100 km (62 miles) from the parent plant.

## FOR THE DEFENCE

Their brilliant yellow flowers make dandelions bee-friendly harbingers of spring, and their young leaves are highly nutritious. Each of the 100 or more individual florets that compose a single flower is pollen-packed, providing food for pollen beetles, bees (honey, bumble and solitary) and hoverflies. When the seeds set they are good food for many birds including goldfinches and house sparrows.

## THE TREATMENT

You'll need to dig deep to get any dandelion root out of the ground completely, and regrowth is quick and easy from any fragments left behind. Because the leaves lie so flat to the ground plants need removing individually from a lawn unless you resort to a selective weedkiller. A systemic formulation such as glyphosate is probably the only way to kill plants off completely, but it is eco-friendly to let them bloom in selected places.

### Effecting a cure

Known to English country folk as 'piss-a-bed' and the French as *piss-en-lit*, dandelion is an effective diuretic used to flush out the kidneys since the 19th century. New research suggests that it could be effective in lowering blood sugar and treating diabetes. Today dandelion is a common ingredient in remedies for obesity and the buildup of toxins.

### Did you know?

* The dandelion – from the French *dent de lion* – is named from its pointed leaf lobes.

* Dandelion flowers invariably close up at night and in dull weather.

* A single dandelion 'clock' contains up to 400 seeds. If you catch one on the wing, make a wish.

* The white latex that exudes from the cut flower stems is being used to develop a new form of natural rubber. Traditionally it was used as a cure for warts.

E

# ENCHANTER'S NIGHTSHADE

*Circaea lutetiana*

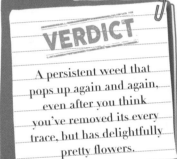

## VERDICT

A persistent weed that pops up again and again, even after you think you've removed its every trace, but has delightfully pretty flowers.

## FOR THE PROSECUTION

Below ground, each enchanter's nightshade plant produces two to six fleshy white shoots (rhizomes), which are not only easily detached but lie dormant over the winter, ready to create new plants in spring. Best of all it likes damp, heavy soil in shade or semi-shade, but will grow almost anywhere. The small hairy fruits are like sticky burrs, easily carried to new territory on clothes or animal fur or skin.

## FOR THE DEFENCE

For the true plant lover, the flowers and fruits of this rather drab looking weed are a delight when looked at closely. The white or pale pink flowers have only two petals, but these are so deeply divided that they look almost like pairs of tiny butterflies. The caterpillars of the elephant hawkmoth feed on the enchanter's nightshade for food after hatching.

## THE TREATMENT

**Vigilance and persistence are key. Plants are very easy to pull out by hand, especially when young, but it's always worth digging down to get rid of as much of the easily visible underground rhizome system as you can. Ideally, remove plants before they have a chance to set seed. For large patches of growth you may need a weedkiller.**

## A story in the name

The Anglo-Saxon name for the plant was *aelfthone*, meaning 'protection from elves', but the name *Circaea*, used from the 16th century, probably relates to Circe, the enchantress of Homer's *Odyssey*, who turned the crew of 'Ulysses' into swine. The species name *lutetiana* may come from *Lutetiani* the old name for Paris, which was once dubbed 'witch city'. Another possibility is that it refers to Paris of Troy, famed for eloping with Helen.

In occult circles the plant is still associated with the enchantment attributed by its English name, and with shape shifting and spells. Among its many alternative names are:

- sorcerer of Paris
- witch's grass
- great witch herb
- wood magic herb

- Paris nightshade
- herb of St Etienne
- St Stephen's wort

Despite its common name, enchanter's nightshade is a close cousin of the rosebay willowherb, and a member of the family Onagraceae and no relation of the deadly and woody nightshades of the family Solanaceae.

# FIELD BINDWIND (OR CONVOLVULUS)

*Convolvulus arvensis*

**VERDICT**

A prettily flowered menace. This bindweed can kill other plants with its powerful grip and invade with its deep, extensive underground root system.

## FOR THE PROSECUTION

So strong is the clinging power of the field bindweed that it is nicknamed 'Devil's guts'. It grows quickly, even from very small pieces of root, and is difficult to remove from both above and below ground. A single field bindweed root system can cover 30 sq metres (35.8 square yards) in a single season and grown downwards over 6 m (20 ft). The small pink flowers do produce some seeds, but these are not its main means of reproduction.

## FOR THE DEFENCE

The flowers, which come in white or shades of pink, are attractive to long-tongued insects, hoverflies and bumblebees. In the right circumstances convolvulus can make an effective cover for a structure such as a basic chicken wire fence. The leaves and stems are nutritious for rabbits and were used as food for them in ancient breeding grounds known as pillow mounds.

## THE TREATMENT

Bindweeds must be dug out before they obliterate your precious flowers and crops such as raspberries, and thoroughness is vital to get rid of every scrap of root. You may need to dig up and clean the roots of decorative plants growing nearby before replacing them. Take care if you try to pull bindweed stems away from leafy supports to avoid unwanted damage and wear gloves – the latex in bindweed stems can be an irritant.

Weedkiller will work, but it needs to be strong, and is best applied in the evening and once flowers have formed. Because nearby plants need protection, try unwinding bindweed stems and laying them flat on the ground before spraying, or put up canes near plants where bindweed can climb, but set sufficiently apart enough for you to attack it. Mulching is an excellent deterrent.

## That's amazing

Bindweed stems curl anticlockwise, unlike the clockwise honeysuckle, a fact used in the comic song 'Misalliance' by Michael Flanders and Donald Swan in 1957.

• The name convolvulus means 'to entwine'.
• The latex in field bindweed stems contains an antiseptic herbicide, which helps to explain why it is so resistant to treatment.

**See also** Greater or hedge bindweed (*Calystegia sepium*).

# GREATER (OR HEDGE) BINDWEED

*Calystegia sepium*

**VERDICT**

A persistent nuisance once established, and difficult to remove permanently from both above and below ground, but essential to a type of hawk moth.

## FOR THE PROSECUTION

Although less deep than those of the field bindweed (see Convolvulus) the persistent roots of the greater bindweed are extremely hard to get rid of and it will regrow from minute pieces of root left in the ground. The winding stems quickly smother plants they entwine, and can even kill them. It will also reproduce from seed.

## FOR THE DEFENCE

The large white flowers of the greater bindweed are attractive in an appropriate place on your plot and the fast-growing stems will quickly cover unsightly garden structures. Greater bindweed leaves provide essential food for the larvae of the convolvulus hawk moth; adult moths feed on the sweet nectar secreted from the flower bases.

## THE TREATMENT

Dig as deeply as you can and take care to remove as many small pieces of root as possible, although it's unlikely that you'll be completely successful. It may be necessary to take out 'good plants' at the same time and untwine the bindweed roots. Take care if you try to pull bindweed stems away from leafy supports to avoid unwanted damage and wear gloves – the latex in bindweed stems can cause skin irritation. Instead, unwind them carefully, as for the field bindweed, and treat them similarly (see Composting Weeds).

## Remarkable qualities

🐛 The white flowers of the greater bindweed were praised by Pliny (CE 23–79) in his *Historia Naturalis*, surmising that ' ... Nature in making this flower were learning and trying her skill how to frame the Lilly indeed'.

🐛 The stunning flowers appear almost luminescent in low light, hence the name of morning glory, although 'evening glory' would be equally apt.

🐛 Children have long loved popping large white bindweed flowers from the red bracts that surround them, chanting 'Granny (or Lazy Maisie) pop out of bed'.

🐛 Greater bindweed seeds have been known to germinate after being in the ground for as long as 40 years.

# GREATER PLANTAIN (OR WAYBREAD)

*Plantago major*

## VERDICT

A remarkably tough weed that can be a nuisance, but not a disaster, on lawns and between paving stones. Birds love to eat plantain seeds.

## FOR THE PROSECUTION

Plantains are extraordinarily able to grow where there appears to be little or no soil and their tough leaves resist constant trampling. They can also lie so flat to the ground that they're untouched by a mower. If left to mature, plants will develop thick, sturdy rhizomes almost impossible to remove intact. Just one plant can make around 15,000 seeds in a single season.

## FOR THE DEFENCE

Small birds – especially sparrows – love plantain seeds and help their dispersal by excreting them undigested, hence the plant's alternative names of birdseed and bird's meat. Crushed plantain leaves work like dock leaves in relieving nettle stings. Young plantain leaves are edible if cooked. They taste rather like mushrooms and are rich in calcium and vitamins A, C, and K.

## THE TREATMENT

Avoid simply cutting off the flower heads, which will stimulate plants to produce side shoots. Plantains are fairly easy to remove by hand when young. A weed knife with a hooked end is a boon for scraping roots from paths and patios. On lawns a narrow trowel, hand fork or similar tool works best (see Tools for weeding).

## More good points

☑ For fun, country children pull out the tough leaf ribs to see who gets the longest 'rat tail'. The tail length is said to represent the number of lies told that day. Or, by pulling out the 'substance' from the ribs leaves are made into 'angels' harps'.

☑ Plantain was one of the nine sacred herbs of the Anglo Saxons believed to have healing powers.

☑ The leaves have been made into poultices and lotions to treat wounds and skin problems, and plantain capsules can help relieve throat and chest infections and may be antibacterial.

## A plant with history

The soil of ancient tracks has revealed that England's plantains, with their super-tough leaves, have been surviving human tread from Neolithic times. When it migrated with early settlers to North America it was nicknamed 'white-man's foot' from its ability to mark out tracks. Plantain seeds 40 years old have been known to germinate successfully; its name comes from the leaf shape which is like the sole of the foot.

# GROUND ELDER (OR GOUT WEED)

*Aegopodium podagraria*

## VERDICT

A nightmare weed with a pungent smell that is almost impossible to get rid of once it takes hold, but which is edible and attractive to bees and beetles.

## FOR THE PROSECUTION

Below ground, at the base of each tuft of leaves, ground elder sends out two to five vigorous underground stems (rhizomes) which are white when young and can grow up to 1 m (around 3 ft) in a single year. From each small swelling or node on the rhizomes a new plant can arise, and in winter, when the leaves have died down – if they do at all – buds form on the rhizomes, ready to sprout as soon as spring arrives.

## FOR THE DEFENCE

Ground elder is edible, being a rich source of vitamin C and antioxidants, while beetles and bees benefit from its umbels of creamy white flowers. Medicinally it has long been known to be effective in treating gout, hence its alternative name; and *podagra*, part of the species name, is Greek for gout. Because it is said to have cured St Gerard of the problem it is also called herb Gerard and bishop's weed. Medicinally it can help to relieve the symptoms of arthritic conditions.

**WARNING!**
Don't ever be fooled into acquiring an allegedly benign variegated variety of ground elder for your garden. Ignore any labelling or mention of pretty white flowers. It will be just as invasive.

## THE TREATMENT

**Constant vigilance and weekly weeding are absolutely essential. If ground elder has grown between decorative plants in a bed or border, dig everything up and wash the roots of the 'good' plants before teasing away all the ground elder. Then clear the ground – dig, dig and dig again – before replacing them. Regular hoeing, which takes off the foliage just below ground level, will weaken plants but is unlikely to kill them, so a systemic weedkiller may well be your only solution.**

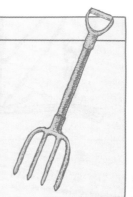

## Apportioning the blame

Ground elder isn't native to Britain, but may have been brought here by the Romans. Or it could have been imported in medieval times as a green vegetable. It certainly featured in monastic gardens but by the time it was first mentioned in print, in Lyte's *Herbal* of 1578, it was already well on the way to becoming a garden plague.

# HORSETAIL (OR MARE'S TAIL)

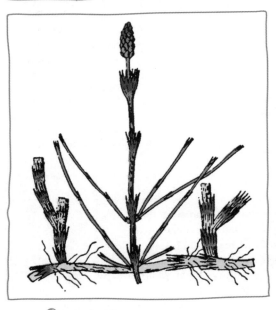

*Equisetum arvense*

**VERDICT**

An ancient non-flowering menace you never, ever, want to find in your garden. Plants are not only virtually impossible to eradicate but poisonous to horses and other grazing animals.

## FOR THE PROSECUTION

The horsetail's hairy, near-black underground stems (rhizomes), which are almost invisible in the soil, penetrate as much as 2 m (6½ ft) beneath the surface. And these produce tubers which can then easily detach themselves – a process assisted by digging – making new plants spring up in what seems to be cleared ground. Take on allotments containing horsetail at your peril.

## FOR THE DEFENCE

Horsetail is a botanical curiosity (see below) with a variety of uses. Its silica-rich stems make traditional polishes for brass, ivory and hardwoods, while wind instrument players use it to condition their reeds. In Japan young fertile stems are cooked and eaten like asparagus in a dish called *tsukushi*. Herbalists recommend horsetail preparations for a range of conditions including rheumatic complaints.

## THE TREATMENT

Getting rid of – or at least controlling – horsetail takes energy and persistence. Deep digging season by season will work to a degree, and help you to cope with minor invasions. Remove new shoots as soon as you see them to help weaken plants. In ten years you may be rid of it! Even strong glyphosate weed killer needs to be applied for several years in succession and success is far from guaranteed.

## An extraordinary life history

Horsetail first appears in spring as small 10 to 25 cm (4 to 10 in) brownish shoots tipped with cones from which minute spores are released by the million. These are then followed by the branched bright green sterile stems from which the names mare's tail, and *Equisetum* from the Latin for 'horse hair', probably arise. And there's no mistaking the distinctive stem sections which can be pulled apart – hence its other names of puzzlegrass and 'Lego plant'.

## An ancient past

Perhaps the success of this rampant flowerless weed lies in its ancient history. More than 100 million years ago, in the Triassic period, the horsetail and its relatives dominated forest understories. Today *Equisetum* is the only surviving horsetail genus and one of the oldest land plants on our planet. Most of all it likes the wet ground redolent of prehistoric forests.

# JAPANESE KNOTWEED

*Fallopia japonica*

## VERDICT

Despite attracting bees, it totally deserves its bad reputation. It smothers other plants, can cause serious structural damage and is controlled by law.

## FOR THE PROSECUTION

Not only can it grow 10 cm (4 in) every day in summer, reaching a height of over 2.1 m (7 ft), but below ground the frost-resistant rhizomes of this knotweed can spread up to 7 m (23 ft) horizontally and 3 m (10 ft) downwards. When cut, it regenerates rapidly and will regrow from pieces as small as 2 mm. It is subject to strict legal controls. (See Weeds and the law).

## FOR THE DEFENCE

Bad growth habits apart, there are good reasons why Japanese knotweed was once appreciated as a garden ornamental. The nectar-rich flowers attract bees and the young leaves make a tasty spinach-like vegetable (but are high in oxalic acid which can aggravate gout, kidney stones, rheumatism or similar conditions). The young rhubarb-flavoured shoots are a prized vegetable in Japan, and are said to strengthen Samurai warriors.

## THE FINAL WARNING!

Garden centres sell a variety of Japanese knotweed named 'compacta', reputed to be less invasive. Don't be tempted. It can run out of control in no time.

## THE TREATMENT

Always call for professional help if you discover Japanese knotweed in or near your garden. For a small invasion you could try a glyphosate weedkiller, re-applied as soon as any regrowth appears, but *never* start digging it out. It must always be safely disposed of under licence, usually granted by your local authority, never composted or put into a garden bin.

## Past, present and future

🌿 When it arrived in Britain (it was recorded at Kew in 1850) Japanese knotweed, with its heart-shaped leaves, spires of white flowers and clusters of bamboo-like stems was welcomed.

🌿 Trouble began when gardeners began discarding pieces into rubbish tips and onto railway embankments, and by 1960 it had spread to every part of Britain, quickly smothering other plants.

🌿 The UK government spends more than £165 million a year for removal of Japanese knotweed and subsequent repairs due to its growth.

🌿 To date, the most effective controls are biological. Promising trials are employing *Aphalara itadori*, an insect whose larvae suck the sap, weakening and killing plants, and the death dealing leafspot fungus *Mycosphaerella*.

L

# LESSER CELANDINE (OR PILEWORT)

*Ranunculus ficaria*

## VERDICT

Pretty flowers in early spring but invasive in beds and borders and a nuisance on lawns.

### FOR THE PROSECUTION

The celandine reproduces easily via clusters of small tubers just below the soil surface, which are easily detached and spread around as you garden. It also produces bulbils – small bulblike swellings that arise where leaf and stem meet (leaf axils) – which can develop into new plants if they reach the soil, and by the seeds packed into cone-like heads.

### FOR THE DEFENCE

In early spring celandines are a godsend to emerging bumble and honeybees, which relish their nectar. Small flies also feed on these sweet secretions. Young leaves, rich in vitamin C, make an excellent salad ingredient. Medicinally they have a long history, right up to the present.

## THE TREATMENT

**Dig out plants by hand, removing as many as the tubers as you can. Plants are trickiest to remove from lawns and unless widespread may not be worth weeding out. For safety, wear gloves when weeding: skin contact can cause blisters.**

## More good points

☑ Probably from their tuber shape, celandines were once used as a cure for piles – hence their alternative name. Today, dried celandine ointment is used for the same purpose, as well as for cooling skin inflammation.

☑ The herbalist Nicholas Culpeper claimed that celandine cured his daughter of scrofula, known as the 'king's evil' (a type of tuberculosis) in just a week.

☑ Celandine juice is an old remedy for curing warts.

## With the weather

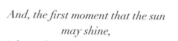

While celandine flowers will stay open while the sun's out they close up in dull weather and in the evening. The poet William Wordsworth (1770–1850) celebrated the flower in his poem 'The Small Celandine':

*There is a flower, the lesser Celandine,*
*That shrinks, like many more, from*
*cold and rain;*

*And, the first moment that the sun*
*may shine,*
*Bright as the sun himself, 'tis out again!*

The naturalist Gilbert White (1720–93) studied celandines around Selbourne, his Hampshire village, concluding that its average date of first flowering was 21 February. Today it often flowers even earlier, especially in southern England.

# LESSER HAIRY WILLOWHERB AND ITS RELATIONS

*Epilobium parviflorum*

## VERDICT

Spreads quickly and easily but its pink flowers are a draw for pollinators. Has many weedy but attractive close relatives, including the rosebay willowherb.

### FOR THE PROSECUTION

These pink-flowered weeds root with ease from their stolons (modified stems) and the wind-borne seeds will germinate in any kind of soil – or even in crevices between paving stones and in walls where there appears to be none.

### FOR THE DEFENCE

The pretty pale pink flowers are attractive to bees, moths and flies. Most notable of its close relations is the rosebay willowherb or fireweed (see opposite).

## THE TREATMENT

**Getting the plants out before the seed-containing capsules can split open and release their contents is key, so it pays to recognize their willow-like leaves (hence the common name). Otherwise you need to pull or dig them out, which for small plants is usually easy as they are not deep rooted. Be careful with composting the roots and stolons (see Composting weeds).**

## The famous fireweed

Originally regarded as a *bona fide* garden plant, rosebay willowherb (*Chamerion angustifolium*) has evolved into a weed of wasteland and larger gardens. Its name of fireweed or bombweed comes from the way it sprang up on the bombsites of World War II, signalling the prospects of new life. Unlike most other willowherbs, which are self pollinating, it is attractive to pollinating bees, wasps and flies, and is the favoured food of the elephant hawkmoth.

Though not very palatable, rosebay willowherb is edible and rich in vitamins A and C and some flavonoids. Medicinally, it is prized by herbalists as treatment for mouth and respiratory problems, including ulcers, bronchitis and laryngitis, and for kidney and urinary tract infections. Creams and lotions containing rosebay willowherb can soothe skin irritations and dermatitis.

## Other common culprits

All these weedy willowherbs flower from June or July into August:

- American willowherb (*Epilobium ciliatum*): Arrived in Britain in the early 1890s. Flowers are small, palish pink with four deeply cleft petals.

- Broad-leaved willowherb (*Epilobium montanum*): Larger, paler, almost mauve flowers. Especially rampant in chalky soils.

- Great hairy willowherb (*Epilobium hirsutum*): Has large, bright pink flowers and a dense covering of hairs. Pollinated by hoverflies or bees; the elephant hawkmoth lays its eggs on the leaves. Also called apple-pie and cherry-pie.

# LORDS-AND-LADIES (OR WILD ARUM)

*Arum maculatum*

**VERDICT**

A fascinating but highly poisonous plant. Decorative in a woodland or shrubby setting but can be a persistent nuisance in beds and borders.

## FOR THE PROSECUTION

Spreads easily by means of tuberous roots and by seeds contained in clusters of fleshy, poisonous, bright red berries. The brown tubers covered with fat, white, hair-like roots, can grow as much as 30 cm (1 ft) below the surface, making them difficult to remove completely. Plants will regenerate from even very small pieces and the seeds germinate easily.

Lords-and-ladies looks attractive in flower and in berry. The fleshy covered seeds are eaten by blackbirds and other garden birds, then pass undigested through the avian intestine before germinating. At night, the spadix (see below) attracts insects and can emit a weak light, which is why the plants are also called fairy lamps or shiners. In Elizabethan times, the crushed roots were used to starch clothes.

## THE TREATMENT

Using a tool such as a daisy grubber on the roots is often a better solution than a trowel or fork. As well as wearing gloves, always keep your hands well away from your mouth, and wash thoroughly after touching any part of the plants, especially the berries. If you need to resort to weedkiller, it's best painted onto individual plants with a brush.

## The unusual flower

Lords-and-ladies has a flower without petals which consists of a club-shaped purplish spadix enclosed within a bright green leafy hood, the spathe. Below the spadix are, in order, a ring of hairs, and clusters of male and female flowers.

By emitting heat, and a smell redolent of decay, the flower attracts owl midges and other flies, which crawl all over the top of the spadix. These are then trapped in the ring of hairs and can escape only by moving downwards to collect pollen from male flowers.

## Sexy connections

The phallic shape of the spadix has given rise to any number of names for lords-and-ladies, which may have come from the saucy expression 'the Lord's and the Lady's'. Among the most expressive are willy lily, Adam and Eve and cows and bulls. Some of the plant's other common names include Jack-in-the-pulpit, Devils and angels, toad's meal and snake's meat.

# RAGWORT

*Senecio jacobaea*

**VERDICT**

A controversial weed most likely to be a pest if you have pasture. Persistent and toxic to horses and cattle but supports a host of insects and other organisms.

## FOR THE PROSECUTION

Ragwort can easily get into allotments and larger gardens. It is spread largely by seed – an average sized plant can produce as many as 100,000 of these contained in hairy fruits borne on the wind like parachutes. And established plants can send roots down to at least 35 cm (15 in). The alkaloids in ragwort are particularly risky for animals when consumed dried in hay (see Weeds and the law).

## FOR THE DEFENCE

Ragwort's striking yellow flowers make large amounts of nectar. It is attractive to at least 77 different insect species, including butterflies and moths, plus other invertebrates and many fungi. Ragwort plants are rarely long lived, making them relatively easy to eradicate. As long as you deadhead it meticulously to stop flowers from setting seed ragwort is worth encouraging in a wild part of the garden.

## THE TREATMENT

If you have just a few plants, dig them out when young, but be conscious that they can grow back from small pieces of remaining root. In wild areas cut them down when they first flower, but always remove these cuttings, bag them up, take them to the tip and declare the contents. A glyphosate weedkiller should be effective in getting rid of ragwort over a season or two.

## Among the visitors

Look for these creatures on or visiting your ragwort:

Caterpillars of the cinnabar moth feed on it voraciously. They can actually control the plant's spread, but in the wild the moth population is declining rapidly.

The black-headed conch moth, the snout moth, the scarce clouded knot-horn moth and the increasingly rare Sussex emerald moth.

The small copper butterfly, the leaf beetle and the picture-winged fly.

## Did you know?

• The species name *jacobaea* refers to St James, patron saint of horses. The plant was once, wrongly, administered to horses suffering from staggers, a disease with symptoms similar to those of ragwort poisoning.

• In Scotland ragwort is called stinking Billy, from the powerful smell exuded when the leaves are crushed, and from William, Duke of Cumberland who defeated the Scots at the Battle of Culloden in 1746.

# RED CLOVER

*Trifolium pratense*

## VERDICT

More to be encouraged than scorned, and well worth cultivating actively for its attractiveness to bees, butterflies and moths and its soil improving abilities.

## FOR THE PROSECUTION

Red clover, which is much less of a garden nuisance than its white cousin, tends to grow in clumps rather than sprawling mats. It is spread mostly by seeds ejected from the bunches of minute capsules that form as the blooms fade. Even without flowers it is easily identified by the pale chevrons on its leaves.

## FOR THE DEFENCE

Red clover is especially attractive to many species of honey and bumble bees, all foraging for the sweet nectar in the bases of the florets. In some places it is even called 'honeysuckle'. Long-tongued flies, butterflies and moths will also feed here. Red clover enriches the soil with the help of its bacteria-filled root nodules which trap and release nitrogen, so is worth growing as a green manure.

## THE TREATMENT

**Dig or hoe out as you wish, ideally before plants set seed. Or simply cut off and compost the plant tops regularly as they mature and leave the roots in the ground to do their good work over the winter. If you must use a weedkiller, try one of the organic types.**

## More good points

☑ The flower heads can be picked, dried and used in infusions and ointments. The resulting preparations have a variety of uses from relieving inflammation both externally and internally, acting as a diuretic, anti-spasmodic and as a treatment for digestive ills.

☑ A clover infusion is an old remedy for whooping cough. However it should <u>only</u> be used under medical supervision.

☑ Both fresh and dried flowers can be made into a potent wine.

☑ Red clover often produces leaves with four, not three, leaflets, which have long been regarded as lucky and have traditionally been worn to ward off witches and warlocks.

## Praise in verse

The American poet Emily Dickinson (1830–86) perfectly summed up clover's sweetest attribute:

*The pedigree of honey*
*Does not concern the bee;*
*A clover, any time, to him*
*Is aristocracy.*

**See also** White clover
*Trifolium repens.*

# SLENDER (OR THREADSTALK) SPEEDWELL

*Veronica filiformis*

**VERDICT**

Pretty blue flowers detract from this speedwell's invasiveness, especially on lawns where it can form dense mats and is resistant to many types of weedkiller.

## FOR THE PROSECUTION

This speedwell quickly produces many runners, allowing it to form dense mats. Even small pieces can generate new plants. When stems are cut into short pieces by the mower they are effectively scattered around the lawn and these too can grow into new plants.

## FOR THE DEFENCE

In informal beds and borders a strong case can be made for allowing speedwells to remain and flower – as long as they are kept under reasonable control. It responds well to being subdued by mulching (see Mulching).

## THE TREATMENT

On lawns speedwell is best removed by hand, although this may not prevent you from inadvertently scattering small pieces of root. Treat weeds in beds with a trowel, hand fork or hoe but use a selective weed killer if absolutely necessary. Don't compost grass cuttings containing speedwell. Collect and take them to your local tip. Letting your grass grow a little longer than normal will help to smother this weed.

## With best intentions

Fancying, correctly, that it would thrive in rock gardens, the plant hunters who found the slender speedwell growing wild in Turkey and the Caucasus brought it to western Europe in the late 19th century. Only in the 1920s did gardeners discover how easily it could escape, and how rampant it could become.

## Speedwell superstitions

• Speedwell was once sewn into travellers' clothes for luck and to 'speed' them on their journeys.
• It's said in country districts that if you pick a speedwell your eyes – or those of your mother – will drop out.

## Weedy relations

✤ The germander or bird's eye speedwell (*Veronica chamaedrys*), has intensely blue flowers. More likely to appear in beds and borders than lawns, it is perfectly able to survive the mower.

✤ The ivy-leaved speedwell (*Veronica hederifolia*) is a trailing annual with tiny flowers which spreads by seed.

✤ The large field or Buxbaum's speedwell (*Veronica persica*), is also annual. Paler petals have dark blue veins.

STINGING NETTLE

S

*Urtica dioica*

## VERDICT

Despite their pain-inflicting qualities, nettles are far from the worst weeds, boasting excellent ecological and nutritional credentials. Well worth accommodating in an informal garden setting.

### FOR THE PROSECUTION

Nettles can spread rapidly below ground using tough yellow rhizomes from which roots emerge at intervals (on nodes). Of course they will sting you on touch as the tips break off their supremely adapted hairs and enter your skin, releasing formic acid as they do so. Unlike some other perennials, nettles produce many seeds, which germinate readily.

## FOR THE DEFENCE

A nettle patch is home to many insects, including 40 overwintering species. These provide food in spring for ladybirds, blue tits and other birds, and all year for hedgehogs, shrews, frogs and toads. Moths and butterflies rely on nettles, notably small tortoiseshells, red admirals and peacocks. Abundant seeds nourish sparrows and finches, young leaves are edible, and excess plants make an excellent fertilizer.

## THE TREATMENT

**Young plants are relatively easy to dig out, but older ones will be easier to handle if you cut them back before you dig and may well need weedkiller treatment if they persist. Always wear gloves and, for tall patches, fully protective clothing. Use cut tops for fertilizer, but be sure to discard the roots.**

## Nettle fertilizer

Make this money-saving nutrient at your own pace.
• **At speed**: steep 30 g (1 oz) nettles in 250 ml (½ pint) of boiling water for 1 hour. Strain and dilute at 1:10 before use.
• **At length**: Fill a large bucket with crushed stems and leaves and weigh down with bricks. Fill to ¾ with water and 'brew' for 4 weeks. Then dilute as above.

## Did you know?

↪ If you have nettles, your soil is nitrogen rich.

↪ The nettle's strong fibres have been used like flax since ancient times.

↪ Romans in Britain stung themselves deliberately to keep warm.

↪ Nettle roots will make a yellow dye, leaves and stems green and brown ones.

## FIRST AID

Avoid pain by 'grasping the nettle', which breaks off the stinging hairs. If you're stung, cucumber or some baking soda, both alkaline, can provide temporary ease (dock leaves incidentally are also acidic). Then rinse with clean, cold water but don't rub. Apply some masking tape, then remove it quickly to pull out remaining hairs, followed by antihistamine cream, aloe vera or calamine lotion.

# WHITE (OR DUTCH) CLOVER

*Trifolium repens*

## VERDICT

A persistent nuisance on lawns but highly valuable for attracting bumble bees, honey bees and other long-tongued insects to your garden and for improving your soil.

## FOR THE PROSECUTION

Spreads with sturdy, creeping stems, which take root as they grow. White clover habitually lies low in a lawn making it impervious to the blades of the mower. It also reproduces effectively with its many seeds, which are able to germinate even after passing through the guts of cattle and other animals.

## FOR THE DEFENCE

White clover produces masses of honey-scented nectar deep inside each of the many tubular florets that compose each flower, attracting bumble and other bees. The flowers can be pulled off and the nectar sucked out, hence its country name of bee-bread. Like red clover it improves the soil by fixing nitrogen using the bacteria in its root nodules.

## THE TREATMENT

Dig or hoe white clover from beds and borders or rake it out of a lawn if you wish, but it is hard to remove and will regrow easily. Letting the grass grow a little longer than usual will give it an advantage over the prostrate clover and help to suppress it. If you must use a weedkiller, try one of the organic types. It may not kill the clover off but will weaken it and make it easier to rake off.

## For the bees

Beekeepers rate white clover as a favourite because it is one of the plants that flowers early in the season, directly after the dandelions, and produces what they term 'main flow' nectar for the hive.

## A weedy relation

The lesser trefoil, *Trifolium dubium* has similar leaves to the white clover, but has yellow flowers, and is an annual, not a perennial. It is also attractive to bees and can be equally virile in a lawn, where it can be treated like its white cousin.

In Irish tradition it is revered as the shamrock believed to have been used by St Patrick to explain the Trinity to his followers. It multiplies itself by seeds, which germinate into rapidly spreading plants with long overground runners.

Other common names for the plant include suckling clover, little hop clover or lesser hop trefoil from the likeness of the faded flower heads to hop fruits.

# WHITE DEADNETTLE

*Lamium maculatum*

**VERDICT**

Pretty flowers in early spring but invasive in beds and borders and a nuisance on lawns.

## FOR THE PROSECUTION

As well as spreading via their rhizomes, white deadnettles also multiply by shedding huge numbers of seeds – a single plant can produce as many as 2,400 seeds, known as nutlets, in a single season. These are likely to drop near the plant, but are commonly carried around the garden by ants. It has a musty smell disliked by some.

## FOR THE DEFENCE

While it looks rather like a stinging nettle when young, this deadnettle's benign characters quickly emerge. Each of the tubular white flowers, borne from May to December, has two distinct lips, the lower one acting as a landing strip for bees, which probe for drops of nectar in the tube bases. Young leaves can be picked and eaten raw in salads or cooked as a vegetable.

## THE TREATMENT

Needs to be carefully dug up, removing all the tough rhizomes, when growing in beds and borders, but worth making a space for in a wilder, sunny part of the garden where it can do great service as a bee magnet, especially early in the year when nectar sources are scarce. If you don't want it to spread, be sure to prevent it from setting seed.

## What's in the name?

The common name of deadnettle is obvious from the absence of stinging hairs, while the generic name (which it shares with the annual deadnettles, including the red-flowered species *Lamium pupureum*) comes from the Greek *lamia* meaning 'monster'. This refers to the shape of the flower, which looks rather like a mouth with wide open jaws.

In country districts the white deadnettle is also known as 'Adam and Eve in the bower', from the way in which the stamens nestle closely together within the flower hood, and as helmet flower and white archangel. The latter relates to its relative the yellow archangel (*Lamistrum galeobdolon*) which is dedicated to the Archangel Michael because it is usually in flower on 27 April, his feast day.

# Garden Thugs

They may look delightful in the garden centre, or be on sale at bargain prices at the village fête, but there are some cultivated specimens that you'll introduce to your plot at your peril. These thugs, the outright garden bullies, have the ability – and if you allow them the opportunity – to become a real nuisance by growing rapidly and reproducing with consummate ease. Once they take hold, garden thugs will involve you in endless work, whether you're cutting them back, coping with their clumps or digging out their progeny.

With the exception of borage, which is an annual spread by seed, all the plants in this section are perennials. Here you'll discover a wide spectrum of reproductive and growing strategies, from the sturdy clumps or culms of bamboo, to the chains or corms formed so readily by crocosmia and the fast growing rhizomes that help Japanese anemones attempt to colonize a complete bed in just a couple of seasons.

On the plus side, fast growers like Russian vine can quickly cover unsightly structures while bamboo and Leyland cypress make almost instant dividers or hedges. Horseradish, Jerusalem artichokes and mint are all invaluable in the kitchen, despite their persistence and propensity for spreading. And it is impossible to resent the butterflies drawn to a buddleia or the bees that hum gratefully around grape hyacinths in early spring or on lemon balm in midsummer. So the choice is yours.

## Quick verdicts

As well as the plants described in detail in this section, there are other potential garden brutes that any gardener should consider carefully, including:

**Hops** (*Humulus lupulus*) – quick cover and attractive fruits making branches perfect for drying and indoor decoration, but can easily rampage.

**Cypress spurge** (*Euphorbia cyparissias*) – spreads with both underground roots and seeds. Useful groundcover but very hard to confine.

**Wild violet** (*Viola odorata*) – wonderful purple colour and a heady scent but its explosive fruits send seeds everywhere, including the lawn where they will germinate and plants stay firmly put.

**Pendulous sedge** (*Carex pendula*) – not only forms brutish clumps that are very hard to dig out but scatters its seeds far and wide.

**Hybrid bluebell** (*Hyacinthoides* x *massartiana*) – pale blue flowers, pink or cream flowers and not a patch on the deep blue of the native British bluebell that was one of its original parents. Spreads rapidly by seed and bulbs.

B

# BAMBOO

*Arundinaria, Phyllostachys* and other running types

## VERDICT

Choose the right type of bamboo and you'll have no problem and garden canes for life. But choose one of the running types and you'll have trouble if your space is confined.

### FOR THE PROSECUTION

Running bamboos reproduce by sending out from their stalks (known as culms) tough, vigorous rhizomes just under the soil surface. They do this particularly productively if your soil is fertile and moist. If buying bamboo, check the label carefully (see opposite), and never buy one without a name, even at a bargain price.

### FOR THE DEFENCE

Bamboo is ideal and attractive for creating camouflage and barriers of all kinds in the garden. You can cut and use it to make your own garden canes and young shoots are edible. Past and present, it has a wide range of eco-friendly uses.

## THE TREATMENT

For small invasions it's possible to dig out the offending rhizomes and cut them back close to the parent, ideally in spring. To control a large spread, work in stages from the edges inwards, probably over several years. First use a spade or shovel to cut through the outer rhizomes to separate them. Cut off the top growth – you may need a lopper or even a chain saw to do this. Repeat.

Once pieces are properly separated, pour boiling water over them. The same treatment is most effective on small pieces of new growth. Use weedkiller with extreme caution – you risk wiping out entire clumps.

If you're in any doubt about which type of bamboo you've bought, grow it in containers or sink in a barrier, either plastic or metal.

### Best avoided

All these bamboo genera are likely to get rapidly out of hand:

- *Arundinaria*
- *Bashania*
- *Chimonobambusa*
- *Clavinodum*
- *Hibanobambusa*
- *Indocalamus*
- *Pleioblastus*
- *Pseudosasa*
- *Sasa*
- *Sasella*
- *Sasamorpha*
- *Semiarundinaria*
- *Sinobambusa*
- *Yushania*

### Many uses

Worldwide, bamboo has an extraordinary number of uses, as well as supporting garden plants of all kinds. These include:

- Scaffolding, bridge building and furniture – bamboo is strong and flexible.

- Medicinally, bamboo extract is used to treat a variety of conditions from kidney disease to cancer.

- Bamboo is excellent for everything from eating utensils to bags and jewellery. Bamboo nappies are both biodegradable and antibacterial.

- Musical instruments made from bamboo are among the oldest and sweetest known.

**L**

# BORAGE

*Borago officinalis*

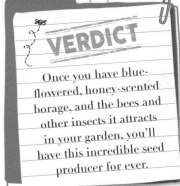

## VERDICT

Once you have blue-flowered, honey-scented borage, and the bees and other insects it attracts in your garden, you'll have this incredible seed producer for ever.

## FOR THE PROSECUTION

This hairy-leaved Mediterranean annual, which blooms most of the year in mild regions, is such an efficient seed producer and germinator that it pops up in the garden again and again … and again. The seeds are so numerous and viable that you'll find yourself removing small plants time after time.

## FOR THE DEFENCE

Borage attracts bees, wasps and many other insects, and makes a great companion plant for tomatoes and brassicas by repelling tomato hornworms and cabbage moths. The leaves have a cool cucumber-like flavour, and it is rich in vitamin C, has medicinal qualities and can make a manure or mulch. The flowers are also edible.

## THE TREATMENT

**Pull, hoe or dig up excess plants well before they set seed and dig them straight back into the ground as a green manure, or lay them on the surface as an instant mulch.**

## EDIBLE DELIGHTS – BUT TAKE CARE!

Enjoy borage, but sparingly and with caution. It contains alkaloids with the potential of causing liver damage and is also carcinogenic. Always select the youngest, most tender leaves for cooking – old ones are tough and bristly.

• Add borage to enhance Pimm's and other gin-based cocktails.

• Use leaves for salads.

• Chop leaves finely and mix with cream cheese or yoghurt.

• Add to other herbs to make a sauce for fish, shellfish or chicken – this is a German favourite known as 'green sauce'.

• Use the flowers in salads or as a garnish.

• Decorate cakes and desserts with flowers dipped in egg white and dried.

## Medicinal benefits

Borage was once valued as a cure for depression. The Greeks and Romans mixed it with wine to 'drive away sadness', and it was similarly recommended by the philosopher and scientist Francis Bacon (1561–1626) and the herbalist John Gerard (1545–1611).

Today's herbalists use borage to treat disorders of the digestive system, lungs circulation and urinary system, but it is most highly valued for the oil in its seeds, often marketed as starflower oil. This is used to treat some skin conditions, rheumatoid arthritis and lung disease.

# BUTTERFLY BUSH (OR BUDDLEIA)

*Buddleja davidii*

## VERDICT

A shrub invaluable for attracting a host of butterflies and bees to your garden, but its seeds will germinate anywhere and everywhere from paving and walls to uncleared gutters.

### FOR THE PROSECUTION

Buddleia has escaped from the shrubbery to become a weed and then returned. It produces vast numbers of winged seeds on the breeze which, when they land, can germinate in the sparsest conditions in and beyond your plot. These have a particular liking for crumbling mortar.

### FOR THE DEFENCE

Among the many butterflies an 'ordinary' pale purple buddleia will attract to its cone-shaped flower heads are peacocks, commas, and painted ladies. In hot summers hummingbird hawk moths arriving from continental Europe will also enjoy its sweet nectar, probing the blooms with their long proboscises.

## THE TREATMENT

**Pull or dig up any unwanted plants before they take hold with tenacious roots. If they've got too big for this, or are squeezed into tiny cracks, a glyphosate weedkiller may be your only alternative. For bushes you want to keep, cut them back as soon as they've flowered. This will prevent the seed from spreading and stimulate new flower formation. Prune them back thoroughly in late winter or early spring.**

## Officially labelled

Because buddleia now grows so extensively outside gardens, particularly on wasteland and railway embankments the UK Department for the Environment, Food and Rural Affairs (DEFRA) has labelled it an 'invasive non-native species', noting that in the wild it will out-compete native vegetation and reduce diversity.

## Asian origins

The French missionary Père David was the first European to see *Buddleja davidii* flowering on the rocky slopes of the China-Tibet border. It reached Kew Gardens in 1896 and quickly became a garden favourite, but in 1922 was first recorded growing wild in Meronieth.

The genus name *Buddleja* was given posthumously in honour of the British naturalist Rev Adam Buddle (1665–1715) by Linneaus who accidentally misspelled the name, using a 'j', not an 'i'. It is also commonly called the summer lilac and the orange-eye.

## Well-bred choices

Plant breeders have strived to produce buddleias with different flower colours, longer flowering seasons and sterile seeds. Those created by Englishman and buddleia expert Peter Moore, include:

'Sugar Plum' – compact with reddish flowers.

'Pink Pagoda' – pale pink flowers.

'Silver Anniversary' – silvery foliage, white flowers and compact habit.

# CROCOSMIA (OR MONTBRETIA)

*Crocosmia* x *crocosmiiflora*

**VERDICT**

Great for filling gaps in the border, and providing bright colour from late summer into autumn. Attractive to pollinators, but can spread readily with the help of its many corms.

## FOR THE PROSECUTION

Crocosmia spreads so widely because its corms not only build up in chains like big, fibrous necklaces, but create many small cormlets, which pop up everywhere as new plants in spring. If allowed to get out of control it will smother groundcover plants, smaller perennials, and even small shrubs. It is illegal to let it stray beyond your garden. (See Weeds and the law).

## FOR THE DEFENCE

Crocosmia blooms come in delightful shades of red, yellow and orange and, because they make good quantities of nectar late in the season, attract both hoverflies and bumblebees. The faded leaves, if you can resist removing them, make excellent shelter for insects over the winter and protect new, emerging shoots in spring.

## THE TREATMENT

**Repeated digging is the only practical solution – plants won't respond well to weedkiller, even if you choose to use it. Once corms are out of the ground, keep them separate with any 'suspect' soil for safe disposal. No homemade compost heap will get hot enough to break them down, and you don't want to replace them accidentally. Healthy plants are very resilient, so you can try digging them out, removing every possible corm and cormlet, then dividing and replacing them.**

## From southern lands

Crocosmia originates from southern and eastern Africa, where it thrives in the grasslands. The apt scientific name comes from *krokos*, the Greek for saffron and *osme*, meaning smell, which describes it excellently. Like saffron it is a source of yellow dye.

The most common garden hybrid is a cross between the species *Crocosmia aurea* and *Crocosmia pottsii*. A key plant breeder in the hybridization process was the Frenchman Victor Lemoine (1823–1911), who was best known for his lilacs and peonies. There are many varieties available, including the *Crocosmia.* 'Lucifer' hybrids, but none are notably less invasive.

The common name montbretia honours the French botanist Antoine Francois Ernest Conquebert de Monbret, who accompanied Napoleon on his Egyptian campaign between 1798 and 1801.

# GRAPE HYACINTH

*Muscari armeniacum*

**VERDICT**

Welcome in spring for its bright blue flowers loved by bees, but will quickly become invasive if planted in rich soil. Best confined to areas where it can become naturalized.

## FOR THE PROSECUTION

Grape hyacinths multiply in two ways, by seed and by producing underground a host of small bulblets from the parent bulb. These can take years to get rid of. Its relation, the deep purple, almost black flowered *Muscari neglectum* doesn't warrant a place in beds and borders either – it will seed itself just as vigorously.

## FOR THE DEFENCE

Its beautiful colour makes the grape hyacinth a worthy addition to beds and borders and it is a valuable early spring source of nectar for bees and for small tortoiseshell butterflies. It also naturalizes very easily in informal settings.

## THE TREATMENT

Even if you dig up unwanted plants the bulblets are very likely to remain in the ground. Ideally, identify and remove any germinated seedlings before they flower (this can take up to four years). Deadhead the flowers as soon as they begin to fade to prevent them from setting seed; pull off the leaves at the same time, rather than waiting for them to die down, so that they don't carry on providing nutrients to the bulbs and bulblets.

## Better choices

If you love grape hyacinths but want fewer problems try these:

- *Muscari latifolium* – dark purple flowers each with a topknot of brilliant blue.

- *Leopoldia comosa* – formerly *Muscari comosum*. The tassel hyacinth, native to Italy and Greece, where the bulbs with a bitter, rather onion-like flavour, are considered a delicacy. They are boiled, then either pickled or preserved in olive oil and are valued as a diuretic and appetite stimulant. Avoid the variety '*Plumosum*' which has sterile flowers that won't attract bees.

- *Muscari macrocarpum*, an unusual choice bearing bright yellow, sweetly fragrant flowers.

## An ancient name

The name *muscari*, from the Greek *muschos*, or musk, relates to the flowers' scent and can be traced to the Flemish botanist Carolus Clusius who recorded it in 1601. In 1753 Linnaeus classified it in as *Hyacinthus muscari*, but only a year later the English botanist Philip Miller designated it as belonging to the genus *Muscari*.

# HORSERADISH

*Armoracia rusticana*

**VERDICT**

Plant horseradish with caution. It's excellent for the kitchen but vigorous, invasive and tolerant of even the poorest soil.

## FOR THE PROSECUTION

Horseradish can take over a large area of a vegetable garden or allotment in no time, so think twice about planting it unless you can keep it confined. And because it can regenerate from very small pieces of root it is almost impossible to eradicate entirely once established.

## FOR THE DEFENCE

The root of horseradish is wonderfully piquant when fresh and, as well as being the traditional accompaniment for beef, also makes a perfect partner for ingredients as diverse as smoked mackerel or salmon, ham and beetroot. It is rich in vitamins, freezes well and can be preserved in vinegar, and has many medicinal qualities.

## THE TREATMENT

If already out of control, digging is the best treatment, although success cannot be guaranteed. Always wear gloves when handling horseradish to prevent it from burning and irritating your skin, and be sure to keep it well away from your eyes. You may need to use a weedkiller to get rid of large expanses.

The ideal way of cultivating – and confining – horseradish is to grow it in pieces of drainpipe about 60 cm (2 ft) long pushed into the ground and filled with a compost and soil mixture. In March plant a piece of root 15 to 30 cm (6 to 12 in) long in each container and use them as they mature. Lift the crop in early winter.

## Pungent properties

❀ Horseradish is rich in vitamins C and B, and in iron, calcium, potassium and phosphorus. It was used on long sea voyages to help prevent scurvy.

❀ It contains essential oils that aid fat digestion.

❀ A horseradish poultice is an old remedy for relieving arthritic and rheumatic pain.

❀ Traditionally, horseradish has been used to treat urinary infections and undue fluid retention.

❀ In cancer research, the powerful enzyme known as horseradish peroxidase extracted from the plant root, is giving promising results.

## An easy recipe

To make a creamy horseradish sauce, soak 15 g (½ oz) grated horseradish in 2 tablespoons of boiling water for 30 minutes then drain. Add 1 tablespoon of white wine vinegar, a pinch each of English mustard powder and caster sugar, 150 ml (5 fl oz) lightly whipped double cream or set yoghurt, and salt to taste.

# IVY

*Hedera helix*

## VERDICT

A superb fast-growing cover for walls, fences or the ground, and a magnet for bees and other wildlife in winter, but needs careful control to stop it from running riot.

## FOR THE PROSECUTION

Ivy won't pull a house down, but you don't want it in your gutters, eaves or cracks in any brickwork. As it clings with its aerial (above ground) rootlets it will rob a tree or other supporting plant of nutrients but it is most likely to kill by its sheer weight – it can have a trunk of its own up to 30 cm (1 ft) across. It is difficult to eradicate completely if large.

## FOR THE DEFENCE

Soft, juvenile, triangular ivy leaves are followed by woody growth bearing larger diamond-shaped foliage, greenish yellow flowers and black fruits. If left to flower and fruit ivy is a nutritional boon to bees in winter, to butterflies and other insects, and to blackbirds, waxwings and many other birds. Its dense foliage creates a protected environment for spiders and small nesting birds like wrens.

## THE TREATMENT

**Prise away clinging stems with a weeding knife or similar tool. Then dig out the ground roots; if a plant has become robust, you'll essentially be trying to kill tree roots. Wear gloves – both leaves and stems can cause skin irritation.**

## Good medicine

Long used to charm away warts and verrucas, and to make bowls from which children were fed to ward off whooping cough, ivy has *bona fide* powers to treat coughs and bronchitis and possibly rheumatism. Ivy extract creams will help to soothe skin conditions – and may even banish warts.

## In history, lore and legend

- Like laurel, ivy was worn as a victory symbol by ancient armies.

- With the holly, it comprises the Christmas duo, but was once thought unlucky if brought indoors.

- Ivy wreaths were hung in cowsheds and dairies as protection from evil and to increase animals' appetites (it is a good winter cattle food).

- Because it clings to vines, and is associated with Dionysus, the god of wine, ivy is said to prevent drunkenness.

## Better choices

Several good ivies are more compact and slower growing, but may be more reluctant to flower. Try:

'Ivalace' – a groundcover variety with very glossy deep green leaves.

'Misty' – leaves variegated in green and white.

'Sunrise' – has yellow leaves and red stems.

# JAPANESE (OR CHINESE) ANEMONE

*Anemone hupehensis, Anemone hupehensis* var. *japonica, Anemone* x *hybrida* and many named varieties

## VERDICT

The reliable pink or white blooms of these perennials last to autumn's end, but plants will spread quickly. It can overwhelm its bedfellows and is hard to control.

### FOR THE PROSECUTION

In open ground, these anemones spread by underground rhizomes or tuberous stems that search relentlessly for more space, bullying their neighbours into submission. They will grow from minute pieces of rhizome, are a particular nuisance in a moist, humid underground environment, and will also reproduce from seed.

## FOR THE DEFENCE

As well as bringing welcome pale shades to the autumn garden, and creating superb displays in large beds, Japanese anemones are an excellent late source of pollen for bees and other insects, particularly flies. They are fine if planted up in large containers sunk into the ground, or confined to raised beds or planting areas created between paving stones.

## THE TREATMENT

Digging is the first line of attack, but it can take three, four or even many more years to get rid of these anemones completely as you are bound to scatter small rhizome sections as you work. Take these out as soon as they spring up as small plants. If you work on large clumps, dig under a few of them to assess whether they're coming from small pieces of broken root or from the original tough and woody dark-coloured roots that are still buried deeply.

For a possibly speedier result, use a full strength glyphosate weedkiller (see Weedkillers and how to use them), but be prepared for plants to be resistant. Take great care to shield surrounding plants from its effects. To stop plants from reproducing by seed, always deadhead them thoroughly.

## A plant with history

Although dubbed 'Japanese', *Anemone hupehensis* is native to Hupeh province in eastern China, but was for centuries a popular flower in Japanese gardens. While first named and described in *Flora Japonica* (1784), by the Swedish naturalist Carl Thunberg, it was the Scottish botanist Robert Fortune (1812–80), who first brought it to Europe. Fortune (notorious for smuggling tea plants out of China) discovered it growing in a Shanghai graveyard and in 1844 sent his first samples of this virtually indestructible plant back to Britain.

# JERUSALEM ARTICHOKE

*Helianthus tuberosus*

## VERDICT

Even in a spacious allotment these artichokes can quickly get out of control. But they can make a good border or windbreak and can be harvested, cooked and enjoyed all winter.

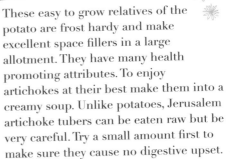

### FOR THE PROSECUTION

Jerusalem artichokes spread by knobbly tubers, of which even the tiniest 'volunteers' can generate completely new plants. Just one plant can produce as many as 200 individual tubers in a single season. Although tasty, they are notoriously flatulent.

### FOR THE DEFENCE

These easy to grow relatives of the potato are frost hardy and make excellent space fillers in a large allotment. They have many health promoting attributes. To enjoy artichokes at their best make them into a creamy soup. Unlike potatoes, Jerusalem artichoke tubers can be eaten raw but be very careful. Try a small amount first to make sure they cause no digestive upset.

## THE TREATMENT

**Persistent digging to get rid of potentially viable tubers of all sizes is all that's needed to keep Jerusalem artichokes under control. While the tops can be composted, beware of getting tubers into your compost where they will almost certainly sprout *in situ*. Make the effort to separate them and add them to your regular food refuse.**

## For your health

* Jerusalem artichokes are great for weight-reducing diets and diabetics, being packed with the soluble carbohydrate inulin, a soluble carbohydrate that can't be digested in the small intestine.

* In the large intestine inulin work as a prebiotic, a perfect food for the bacteria that help to keep the colon in good health.

* Other nutritionally vital ingredients include vitamin C, plus B vitamins niacin, thiamine and riboflavin.

* Among many key minerals the tubers contain are potassium, magnesium, iron, copper and molybdenum.

## Cutting the confusion

Jerusalem artichokes are a type of sunflower native to North America (the globe artichoke is an aristocratic thistle) and are named from the Italian '*girasole*', meaning sunflower. To avoid confusion some suppliers are renaming them 'sunchokes'. Other popular names include sunroot, earth apple and topinambour which comes from Tupinambá, the name of the South American people known to have eaten them centuries ago.

L

# LEMON (OR BEE) BALM

*Melissa officinalis*

**VERDICT**

Admirable for its bee-attracting citrus scent, but has only average looks and spreads far and wide with its shallow roots and copious seeds.

## FOR THE PROSECUTION

Generally uninspiring to look at, lemon balm is naturally invasive and spreads long distances with shallow roots, similar to those of mint, its family relation, and by copious seeds which will quickly germinate and mature in even the poorest or wettest soil.

## FOR THE DEFENCE

As well as attracting bees, lemon balm leaves can help to deter mosquitoes. Its bright green young leaves make a tasty flavouring for food and drinks, and it offers a range of medicinal properties.

## THE TREATMENT

Let lemon balm flower for the sake of the bees, but cut it back well before it seeds. As a bonus you'll get a second growth of fresh leaves in late summer. Pull or dig out any seedlings as you see them. Root spread is best checked in the autumn, and again in the spring. To keep it contained, plant it in big pots, sunk into the ground if you wish.

## A healthy history

🍃 Lemon balm is native to the Mediterranean and the genus name *Melissa* is Greek for honeybee.

🍃 In ancient Greece and Rome sprigs of the lemon balm were put into beehives to attract new swarms to enter. It was also planted around the hives themselves.

🍃 Lemon balm was an essential in the monastery garden for its healing properties. It was used to soothe and treat wounds and skin infections such as herpes.

🍃 An infusion of lemon balm leaves, fresh or dried, can help to relieve indigestion. It can also help to treat mild insomnia and even lift the mood.

🍃 Today, lemon balm is grown commercially for extraction of the essential oil it contains.

## In the kitchen

Try lemon balm in a stuffing, stir fry, risotto or salad, in a lemon sauce for chicken, fish or a dessert, or in a lemon cake or ice cream. It is also a refreshing substitute for mint or borage in Pimm's or other cocktails.

## A better choice

For a lemon scent and less invasion, try the lemon verbena (*Aloysia triphylla* aka *Lippia citriodora*). However it is not fully hardy so will need winter protection.

L

# LEYLAND CYPRESS (OR LEYLANDII)

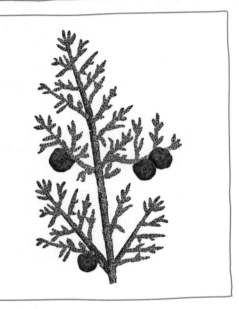

X *Cuprocyparis leylandii*

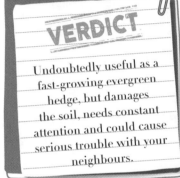

**VERDICT**

Undoubtedly useful as a fast-growing evergreen hedge, but damages the soil, needs constant attention and could cause serious trouble with your neighbours.

## FOR THE PROSECUTION

Because Leyland cypress can grow up to 1 m (3 ft) or more each year it needs constant cutting back. What's more it creates deep shade and sucks the soil dry making it virtually impossible to grow other plants nearby. At the worst it can lead to legal problems if you let it get out of hand (see Weeds and the law).

## FOR THE DEFENCE

Solid, dense and sturdy, and certainly more attractive and providing of more privacy than a plain wooden fence, Leyland cypress does have the advantage of providing a nesting site for many small birds and protection for hedgehogs. When you've cut back or removed Leylandii, all the excess growth can be shredded and used on the garden as weed-deterring mulch (see Mulching).

## Well met?

Leylandii arose from a cross between two American conifers that would not normally come into contact: the fast-growing but quite delicate Monterey cypress (*Cupressus macrocarpa*) and the hardy Nootka cypress (*Chamaecyparis nootkatensis*). In the 19th century both were brought to Britain and Ireland by plant hunters. While the first cross took place in Rostrevor, County Down in 1870, the plant is named for Mr Leyland of Leighton Hall in Wales who made a successful cross in 1888. All today's plants come from cuttings dating back to the originals.

## THE TREATMENT

Put on gloves to avoid skin irritations. Trim a hedge you want to keep up to three times between April and August, and don't let it exceed about 3 m (9 ft). When plants are young, concentrate on cutting back the side shoots to create dense growth; cut the top only once until it's the height you want. On mature plants don't cut into leafless growth – this will never produce new foliage.

To get rid of a Leylandii hedge, first decide whether you need professional help – if only with winching out the stumps. To do it yourself, wait until the autumn or winter and cut back to stump level then, as soon as possible, apply a stump killer containing glyphosate and cover each stump with plastic sheeting to keep the rain off. Reapply as necessary (see Weedkillers and how to use them).

Instead of removing Leylandii stumps, think of using them decoratively, for instance with nasturtiums growing over them.

# MINT

*Mentha* x *piperita* – and other species and varieties

## VERDICT

An essential garden perennial for any cook, but mint demands effort and even ingenuity to keep it under control wherever you plant it.

## FOR THE PROSECUTION

Mint spreads speedily with an underground rhizome system, (from which roots grow) and will quickly get out of control. It will flourish even in bone dry soil.

## FOR THE DEFENCE

Versatile in the kitchen and garden, mint is great for covering a wild or scrubby area that would otherwise be uncultivated. Perfect for a fresh tea and has many health giving properties. Its scented flowers are a magnet for bees.

## THE TREATMENT

**Dig out unwanted rhizomes in autumn and again in spring as you see new growth appearing. Best of all, use these methods to keep it under control:**

**• Plant in a container big enough to allow some spread, but because plants quickly get pot bound and straggly in the centre, be prepared to dig up, divide and re-pot it every couple of years.**

**• Use a 'shield' of metal or plastic edging to create a confined area but make sure that this is buried deeply enough – ideally 30 cm (1 ft) – to keep roots confined. Or dig in one or more large biscuit tins with plenty of holes pierced in the base before planting.**

**• Plant in a series of large diameter drainpipe sections.**

## Many merits

• The taste of mint is a perfect partner for lamb, potatoes, peas and essential in a tabbouleh. It will heighten the flavour of fruits such as melon, strawberry and lemon.

• It is extremely effective in soothing dyspepsia, especially in an infusion of dried leaves.

• The menthol mint contains is a mild anaesthetic and an antidote to bee and wasp stings.

## Did you know?

• In Roman legend Proserpine, wife of Pluto, the commander of the underworld, changed her rival into a mint plant.

• Mint, native to southern Europe, probably came to Britain with the Romans.

• From the 14th century mint has been used in toothpaste to sweeten the breath and to help whiten the teeth.

• Apart from spearmint there are other good mints such as hairy-leaved apple mint, lemon mint and eau de cologne mint whose foliage is a deep greenish purple. Unusual, and less rampant (though more susceptible to frost) are ginger, orange and pineapple mints.

**R**

# RUSSIAN VINE (OR MILE–A–MINUTE)

*Fallopia baldschuanica
(Polygonum baldschuanicum)*

## VERDICT

An aptly named hardy perennial, attractive to bees. It will quickly cover any unsightly garden feature, but equally rapidly rampage. Consider confining it to one or several good-sized pots.

### FOR THE PROSECUTION

Russian vine will grow at around 4 m (13 ft) in a year, quickly reaching a height of 12m (40 ft), and considerably more in width. It can even tear down unstable structures with its strong, clinging tendrils.

### FOR THE DEFENCE

Russian vine is highly attractive to bees throughout its flowering season from May to September. And it will flower most profusely in poorer soil; in a rich environment it will make more foliage than blooms.

## THE TREATMENT

For a plant you want to keep, prune it well and often. To remove it, cut and dig, cut and dig. This may get rid of it in a year or two, but if it has created a trunk then you'll almost certainly need weedkiller to kill it off completely. The experts recommend that you first drill holes in the stump before squirting in a strong glyphosate product. Repeat this as necessary. If using a systemic weedkiller on the leaves, crush some of them first – they have a waxy coating which prevents the chemical from being absorbed.

### In its native land

As its name suggests this vine is native to Russia, but grows naturally in a wider area that includes China and Kazakhstan. Some taxonomists recognize two distinct species, *Fallopia baldschuanica*, from Russia and central Asia and *Fallopia aubertii* from China. Other common names include Chinese fleecevine, Bukhara fleeceflower and silver lace vine.

### WARNING!
Before spraying, make sure that the plant's roots are actually in your garden. You don't want to risk inadvertently destroying a plant belonging to your neighbour.

### Better choices

Any of these climbers will act as excellent camouflage without running out of control:
• *Clematis montana* –vigorous and hardy, but choose the pink, not the white variety.
• *Lonicera henryi* – a pretty honeysuckle with a heady scent.

• Virginia creeper (*Parthenocissus quinquefolia*) – self-clinging and has wonderful red colouring in the autumn, but is deciduous.
• Wisteria – rewards with beautiful inflorescences after a few years. For quickest growth choose *Wisteria sinensis*, the Chinese blue wisteria. Attractive to bees.

# STAG'S HORN SUMACH

*Rhus typhina*

**VERDICT**

Can look wonderful in a large garden, especially in autumn, but sends out vigorous suckers that can be disastrous if they invade your lawn.

## FOR THE PROSECUTION

This large shrub or small tree, brought to Europe from its native North America in the 17th century, has absolutely no place in a small garden. Its suckers pop up as new plants all around the parent, greedily seeking for nutrients. And the milder the winter, the more likely the suckers are to appear.

## FOR THE DEFENCE

With its fiery red, orange or yellow displays of dissected autumn foliage, downy antler-like stems and branches, conical flowers and edible fruits, sumach has many desirable qualities. Because plants are either male or female, choose the latter, which has crimson flowers blooming from May to July maturing in autumn to dense clusters of red berries.

## THE TREATMENT

There is no easy cure for sumach suckers, but the best solution is to keep ahead of the plant by digging out the suckers one by one. The key is to cut through the root linking the sucker to the parent plant. Above ground, cut suckers down to just above ground level and brush on a strong weedkiller intended for tree stumps, ideally when the culprits are as young as possible. You may never get rid of the suckers completely, but in five or six years you may have them under reasonable control. Dispose of the suckers at your local tip or burn them if you can.

Alternatively, try sinking paving slabs vertically around the parent plant to prevent the suckers (which are quite shallow) from spreading.

### What's in a name?

• The stag's horn sumach is named from its velvety, branched stems forked like the antlers of the male deer and covered with rust-coloured hairs.

### Acceptable features

An attractive, less rampant traveller is the variety 'Laciniata' or 'cutleaf' (also sold as 'Dissecta') with finer, more filigree foliage.

The tannin-rich leaves and stems of the sumach have long been used in making natural dyes and as a mordant or fixative in the dyeing process.

# Dealing
## *with*
# Weeds

However you decide to handle your weeds you need to be sure that you are treating them efficiently, safely and legally. It also helps to know how to prevent them from growing in the first instance, and how to redeploy them as compost or green manure to improve your soil. These pages, which end with a handy explanation of some botanical terms, complete the background knowledge that will enhance the individual entries included in the book.

## TOOLS FOR WEEDING

Every gardener needs good tools for weeding and rooting out weeds by hand, rather than using weedkillers, as it is essential to gardening organically. Your aim is always going to be to get every part of the weed out of the ground.

When selecting a weeding tool, always hold it in your hand to check the grip, weight and balance. Many of today's tools come with a choice of short or long handles, or even telescopic ones, an important consideration if you have knee or back issues. New designs come onto the market every season, but there is nothing like an 'old faithful'.

As well as the tools described here, you'll need:

- Gloves – ideally a thin pair that will give you 'feel' and thick ones for dealing with tough, prickly or irritating subjects, and with grasses which can cut you badly.
- A kneeler or low seat.
- Secateurs, shears and possibly a saw and a strimmer.

**Hands** Usually best combined with a tool. Hand pulling always risks leaving a root, rhizome or similar reproductive structure below ground, ready to regenerate.

**Trowel** A hugely versatile tool that comes

in variable widths. For tight weeding a narrow design is often more useful.

**Fork** The hand fork is ideal for removing small weeds. A full-sized fork will serve you well when digging over a larger area, while an old kitchen fork will effectively tease out weeds from between seedlings. The 'prong', a type of fork without inner tines, is useful for grabbing clumps of roots or thicker branches of bigger weeds before levering them out.

**Weeding knife** Available in a variety of designs, but most versatile when it has a hooked end. Extremely useful for removing weeds from between paving stones, and from walls and rockeries.

**Dandelion digger and its variations** The dandelion digger is a metal tool with an inverted 'v' cut in the end and is handy for removing individual weeds of all kinds from a lawn. Variations include the claw, the puller and the twister. These can work well for the gadget lover, but it could be wise to borrow one and see how it works for you before spending your money.

**Daisy grubber** Similar to a dandelion digger, but with a longer, more deeply cleft blade. Stab it into the ground close to the weed then lever it upwards. You may need to lift up the plant leaves by hand before inserting the tool.

**Hoe** An ideal weeding tool in a range of designs, many available with short handles.
- The paddle or draw hoe – has a rectangular blade set at 90 degrees to the handle. Used by pulling it towards you. Good for dislodging all kinds of weeds at the root.
- The stirrup, loop or shuffle hoe – has a blade shaped like a stirrup and can be moved effectively both towards and away from you. Disrupts the soil less than the paddle hoe.
- The Dutch or warren hoe – similar to the paddle hoe but with a triangular blade. Good on stubbornly rooted weeds.
- The onion or collinear hoe – has a long, thin blade that fits neatly into narrow spaces. As well as onions, it is excellent for weeding closely planted rows of young plants.

**Spade** The go-to tool for tackling large expanses of weeds and for deep-set roots. Comes in various widths.

**Mattock** A good old-fashioned tool for really heavy work such as shifting the roots of overgrown Leylandii or ivy.

**Flame gun** Gets rid of weeds on paving, patios and drives by simply burning them off. Always wait for weeds to be thoroughly dry before you use it, wear gloves and take great care not to damage nearby plants or flammable material.

# COMPOSTING WEEDS

Having made great efforts to remove weeds from your garden the last thing you want to do is put them back again in homemade compost. Any annual weeds that haven't gone to seed can be put into the regular compost heap, but any with seeds – and all the perennial weeds – need special treatment to make sure that they are completely dead before their nutrients are recycled.

## HOW TO DO IT
All of these methods should work well:

### 'Normal' composting
Reserve a specific plastic composting bin for perennial weeds. They can be mixed with other vegetable matter, which will help to accelerate rotting. It will take two or three years for them to rot down and you must check that they have decomposed down completely before you use them on your plot.

Alternatively put the weeds into biodegradable bin bags and leave them outdoors – behind a shed for example – covered with a sheet or two of black plastic to keep out light and air. Leave until thoroughly rotted.

### Hot composting
If you can get your compost heap hot enough it will kill off both weed seeds and reproductive organs such as rhizomes and runners. Mix green and brown ingredients in a compost bin placed in a sunny situation. Turn the

## WARNING!
Never, ever, compost horsetail, lesser celandine, bindweed or Japanese knotweed (see Weeds and the law). If in doubt, contact your local authority.

heap often. With luck you will have weed free compost within a year. If not, just be patient.

### Weed soup – the drowning method
This is easy to do and provides the bonus of a liquid fertilizer.
1. Pile perennial weeds into a large bucket and fill with water.
2. Weigh down with bricks or stones to cover the weeds completely.
3. Cover with black plastic or other light-proof material to prevent rainwater entering.
4. Leave for about 4 weeks.
5. Strain off the liquid and use immediately on growing plants diluted 5 to 1 with water.
6. Put the now dead weeds onto the compost heap. If not dead, bag up, as above.

### Desiccation
In hot weather, lay out the weeds in a thin layer on a corrugated shed roof or concrete path. Leave for two or three weeks until dead, then compost as normal. This method makes a majority of weed seeds unviable.

### Bagging
If you have a lawn, use strong plastic bags like this:
1. Mix perennial weeds and grass cuttings in equal quantities.
2. Tie up the bags and leave in a sunny place.

3. After 3 or 4 weeks check that roots have rotted completely.
4. Tip into the compost heap.

### The Japanese revolution
The bokashi bin system is the latest composting technique invented in Japan and now available (although expensive) in the UK. It uses bran inoculated with bacteria which rot the weeds, giving you a continuous supply of liquid fertilizer and dead plants that can be dug into the ground.

### The last resort
If you don't have the space for composting, bag up weeds and take them to your local tip where they will be given high temperature treatment. Always declare any weeds subject to legal controls.

# MULCHING

**For mulching think smothering. Mulches work by depriving weeds of the light essential for growth. As a bonus they may warm the soil and, if organic, feed plants as they decompose.**

## SAFETY FIRST

Many mulches, particularly bark and manure, can be very heavy and lifting them can strain your back. Decanting from bag to wheelbarrow is always sensible. Lay heavy mulches onto the soil in small quantities and wear gloves, especially when handling manure or bark.

### Before you begin

As well as excluding light, mulches (except geotextiles) create a largely waterproof soil covering so always water very thoroughly before a mulch is applied. If you're mulching close to plants that need frequent or copious watering, sink in one or more watering spikes. You can buy these or make your own from discarded plastic bottles.

## THE MOST RELIABLE CHOICES ARE:

### Bark

Comes in various grades – your choice will depend on where you're using it. Most essential is to make sure it's laid on thickly enough. If too shallow it will quickly erode or rot, letting weeds through. Aim for a layer of at least 5 cm (2 in) and preferably more.

### Wood chippings

Can be bought or home produced from branches and the like. Use like bark.

### Sawdust

Readily available from sawmills. Lay in a 5 cm (2 in) layer. Can deplete the soil of nitrogen as it rots, so fertilize as necessary. Excellent on unpaved paths.

### Grass cuttings

Small quantities laid 5 cm (2 in) thick will work, but can get slimy and are best mixed with wood chippings. As they rot, fork them into the soil. They won't be organic if treated with a non-organic weedkiller.

### Leaves or pine needles

Collect these and apply as a 5 to 7.5 cm (2 to 3 in) mulch. Leaves, ideally shredded, will rot down slowly but can be topped up each autumn. They will also work well mixed with bark, wood chippings or straw.

### Straw

Useful in the vegetable garden and allotment, but tedious to apply and liable to blow away on a windy site. It needs to be at least 15 to 20 cm (6 to 8 in) thick.

### Compost or manure

If using your own compost, be doubly sure that it's free of perennial weed pieces and weed seeds. Farm manure can be excellent, but is unlikely to be totally weed free. Lay to a depth of 5 to 7.5 cm (2 to 3 in) or reduce this by half and put chopped leaves on top.

## INORGANIC MULCHES

Technological advances have greatly improved inorganic mulches, making them extremely versatile. Many are also light and easy to handle, but will probably need to be weighted down to keep them in place.

### Newspaper or cardboard

Best used beneath organic mulches such as bark. You'll need at least six sheets of paper or two or three of cardboard for this to be effective. Some gardeners worry about the lead content of newsprint; for safety choose black and white pages only.

### Stones, pebbles or small tile pieces

Ideal for smaller areas such as rockeries and as pot toppers. They come in attractive colours and shapes but are invariably heavy to handle.

### Plastic

Despite its unattractive looks (although it can be covered with a thin layer of bark or wood chippings), plain black plastic is an excellent mulch and can raise the temperature of the soil by as much as 8°C. This is great in spring, but can be damaging in hot weather. Always avoid putting black plastic around shrubs – their roots are shallow and will suffer from a lack of oxygen. When planting out or transplanting, make holes in the plastic for easy insertion.

Look out for the newest infrared transmitting (IRT) plastics which warm the soil even better than plain black plastic.

### Geotextiles or landscape fabrics

These fabrics let air and water into the soil but need replacing regularly as they degrade. Like plain black plastic they may need a decorative covering in the flower garden. Remember that weeds can grow into the mulch itself, making it tricky to remove.

### Old carpet

Covering a larger weedy area with old carpet (ideally not rubber backed) for a year or more is a good way of clearing the ground, and can work as a mulch on smaller uncultivated areas. If you have an allotment, check that carpet use is permitted.

# WEEDKILLERS AND HOW TO USE THEM

**However energetically you pull and dig, mulch and mow, weedkillers are sometimes the gardener's only solution. What's important is to use them sparingly and safely so as not to endanger the health of your 'wanted' plants, you personally, or the environment.**

All weedkillers (herbicides) on sale in the UK will have been tested and declared safe as long as the maker's instructions are followed to the letter. The names of the key ingredients must be included on the label, but is often printed in very small type. These are discussed in detail below.

## KNOW THE RULES

- Don't buy or use a weedkiller until you've read the label. Stick to small quantities and renew as necessary.
- Choose a product provided in a spray or buy one or more spray bottles if you're using a diluted concentrate.
- Always follow timing instructions provided with the product.
- Never spray on a windy day.
- Avoid spraying if rain is forecast within 24 hours.
- Protect your hands with rubber gloves; take care not to inhale any spray.
- Wash with clean water immediately if weedkiller gets onto your skin or into your eyes.
- Protect nearby plants from spray – pieces of corrugated cardboard make excellent plant 'shields' and can be thrown away after use.
- Use the minimum amount at each application, but be sure that a weed is thoroughly covered (including both sides of leaves). It's better to re-spray if necessary.
- Take care that children and pets are not exposed to any weedkiller until it has dried thoroughly.
- Store weedkiller where children cannot possibly reach it – in a locked cupboard if necessary.
- Never decant weedkiller into unlabelled bottles or jars. Keep all containers tightly sealed.
- Clean any utensils immediately after you've used them.
- Don't put weeds treated with non-organic weedkiller onto the compost heap if you are gardening organically.

## WHAT WEEDKILLERS CAN DO

Weedkillers work in a variety of ways depending on the chemicals they contain, but will almost certainly be most effective when plants are in an active state of growth. Selective weedkillers work on only certain types of plants, such as broad-leaved species, while systemic ones work by penetrating the plant, so allowing them to operate right down to root level.

The descriptions below give a general idea of the weedkillers currently available, but new formulations are being marketed all the time, so double check before you begin. Some, especially those formulated for lawns, come with a fertilizer added.

### Organic weedkillers

The best organic weedkillers are those containing pelargonic acid, a natural chemical found in geraniums (pelargoniums). It works by destroying the cell walls of foliage and leaves no harmful residues in the soil. However it is non-selective. Vinegar can also work organically (see 'From the kitchen').

For moss on lawns, products are available containing bacteria that break down the moss naturally, but you need to check on any other ingredients in the mix (such as fertilizer) to be sure that they are organic.

### Selective or 'hormone' weedkillers

These work by targeting only broad-leaved weeds such as dandelions and thistles, not narrow-leaved grasses, which makes them ideal for lawns. They work by mimicking the actions of plant hormones (auxins) which, after being applied to the leaves, travel down to the live roots. As they work, the weed foliage twists and shrivels.

Typical ingredients of these weedkillers, often used in combination, include:

- 2,4 D (2,4 dichlorophenoxyacetic acid) – good for getting rid of dandelions, plantain and clover, and for 'injecting' into stumps. There is divergent opinion regarding its risk as a carcinogen.
- Dicamba (3,6-dichloro-2-methoxybenzoic acid) – usually used in combination with other chemicals. Can stay in the soil for up to six weeks. Used in lawn weedkillers.
- MCPA (2-methyl-4-chlorophenoxyacetic acid) – effective against thistles and docks but many clovers are resistant to it. Contained in many lawn weedkillers.
- Clopyralid (3,6-dichloro-2-pyridinecarboxylic acid) – one of the few chemicals able to kill the creeping thistle (see *Cirsium arvense*), but will cause rapid death to tomatoes and peas, and persist for long periods in the ground.
- Mecoprop-P or MCPP (methylchlorophenoxypropionic acid) – best for treating clovers and

chickweed. Always combined with dicamba in garden weedkillers. A common formulation for lawn weedkillers.

- Fluroxypyr – a synthetic plant hormone, routinely added to many lawn weedkillers.
- Triclopyr (3,5,6-trichloro-2-pyridinyloxyacetic acid) – best suited for use on rough grassland, not the ordinary garden.

### Contact, non-selective weedkillers

As their name suggests, these weedkillers will kill any plant they touch.

- Diquat – the most common, quickly desiccates weeds, killing the foliage, but will not kill off roots, rhizomes or other underground reproductive plant organs. It is highly toxic and can linger in the ground for many years after use. Employ only in extreme circumstances.
- Acetic acid – destroys cell membranes, causing plants to die of desiccation. Although it can be produced by natural fermentation, in most commercial weedkillers it is manufactured and therefore not truly organic. To be effective it must be used in concentrations of between 15 and 30 per cent.
- Ferrous sulphate – commonly used to kill moss on lawns.
- Maleic hydrazide – often used in combination with pelargonic acid. It has the advantage of breaking

down quickly in the soil and adding nitrogen in the process.

### Systemic weedkillers

Individual gardeners will make their own minds up about whether or not to use glyphosate, but 'sparingly' should always be the watchword whenever it reaches the garden.

Glyphosate is the controversial ingredient contained in systemic weedkillers. As it travels throughout the plant it kills by inhibiting protein formation. Glyphosate is undoubtedly effective, but there are serious claims about its toxicity to humans, animals and microorganisms, including earthworms and the mycorrhizal fungi essential to the growth of plant roots. There is also conflicting evidence about how long glyphosate will stay in the soil before breaking down, and how this changes with temperature. And because it is not selective it will rapidly kill any other plants with which it comes into contact.

Glyphosate is contained in most stump killers formulated for 'injecting' into the woody remains of ivy, Leylandii and the like.

### Residual weedkillers

These are formulated to remain in the soil for long periods – often several months – and should only ever be used on hard surfaces. As well as glyphosate they contain diflufenican, which kills plants by ridding them of chlorophyll.

**From the kitchen**
- Boiling water – burns off weed foliage but unlikely to touch the roots. Excellent on paving on patios.
- Cooking vinegar (usually 5 per cent concentration) – an acceptable organic weedkiller, but only truly effective on young plants with tender, non-waxy foliage. (For these, add a few drops of washing up liquid.)
- A salt solution – good on paths and paving but will severely damage the soil in beds and borders, preventing plant growth.

# LAWNS

With a lawn, your choice may be between having a perfect patch of green or a wildflower meadow. The most common lawn weeds are dandelions, clover, daisies, buttercups, speedwell and thistles, plus moss and coarse grasses such as couch. All of them survive because they lie flat to the ground and so resist close, regular mowing. The perennials generally spread themselves with creeping stems or rhizomes, the annuals by seed.

## PREVENTION
- Mow regularly, but don't cut the lawn too short, which can weaken the grass and create bare patches which weeds will quickly colonize.
- Feed a lawn in spring and autumn, and possibly also in summer, to encourage good grass growth. Clover, because it releases nitrogen from its roots, thrives best in poor soil.
- Apply garden lime in winter if your soil is acid.
- Aerate the lawn by spiking it with a fork or a specifically designed aerator between October and March.
- Scarify – rake out dead vegetation – in late spring.

## THE TREATMENT
Getting rid of lawn weeds can be backbreaking and time consuming. These are the best methods to try.

### By hand
You can dig out lawn weeds by hand as they appear, but this will leave bare patches that new weeds will quickly reoccupy. It pays to remove them when they are as young as possible. You can try reseeding patches at any time from spring to autumn.

### Weedkillers
Take care. It is very easy to ruin a lawn with the wrong weedkiller or the wrong

dose. And some lawn weeds, including the slender speedwell (see Slender (or Threadstalk) speedwell) are weedkiller resistant. You are likely to have to give lawn weeds two or more treatments. (For formulations see Weedkillers.)

**In extreme circumstances ...**
No selective lawn weedkiller yet exists that will kill couch or other unwanted grasses such as the annual (but often short-lived perennial) meadow grass (*Poa annua*). If all else fails you may need to kill off all the grass, dig thoroughly to remove all dead roots and rhizomes – and any remaining live ones – before reseeding or re-turfing.

## Always read the label

### Application
Follow these guidelines for weedkiller use on the lawn.

• Apply only when weeds are growing.
• Use in the evening to avoid strong sunshine.
• Choose a day when there is no wind.
• Don't use on completely dry grass or when rain is due within 6 hours or more.
• Wait 2 to 3 weeks after fertilizing before use.

• Don't apply until 3 days after mowing, then wait to mow until at least 3 or 4 days after application.
• For young broad-leaved weeds, carefully spot treat with a selective or broad spectrum weedkiller, but be sure to protect the surrounding grass. Using a paintbrush to apply the weedkiller is a good method of application.
• For the whole lawn, wait until late spring when lawn growth is fully established. Then reapply in the autumn.

# WEEDS AND THE LAW

There are a few weeds that are so harmful to the environment that their control is governed by United Kingdom law.

## THE WEEDS ACT, 1959

This legislation prevents the spread of the following weeds on private land and allows anyone disobeying the law to be fined up to £1,000 and to receive further punishment such as an ASBO (Antisocial Behaviour Order).

**Broad-leaved dock** (*Rumex obtusifolius*)
**Curled dock** (*Rumex crispus*)
**Creeping thistle** (*Cirsium arvense*)
**Ragwort** (*Senecio jacobaea*)
**Spear thistle** (*Cirsium vulgare*).

Your legal obligation is to:

- Prevent them from spreading to agricultural land, particularly grazing areas or land used to produce forage, such as silage and hay.
- Choose the most appropriate control method for your site. You may need to seek permission for certain control methods, especially if your land is a protected site.
- You must not plant them in the wild.

In England and Wales, ragwort is also subject to an amendment of 2003, The Ragwort Control Act, which gives the government powers to provide guidance on how to prevent this weed from spreading. Following objections to the original legislation from wildlife organizations the Code now states that it 'does not propose the eradication of common ragwort but promotes a strategic approach to control the spread of common ragwort where it poses a threat to the health and welfare of grazing animals and the production of feed or forage.'

### Japanese knotweed

Under the Wildlife and Countryside Act of 1981 it is an offence '… to plant or otherwise cause (*Fallopia japonica*) to grow in the wild'. Equally, the plant is classed as 'controlled waste' in the UK. If you fail to control it, or allow it to spread to a neighbouring property, you may be liable for considerable damages. Japanese knotweed must always be safely disposed of under licence, usually granted by your local authority, never composted or put into a garden bin.

Since 2013 the seller of any property is obliged to declare Japanese knotweed if present. This makes it wise to take legal advice, and possibly insurance, as long as you've used professional services for its removal.

### Himalayan balsam

Another immigrant weed covered by the Wildlife and Countryside Act of 1981, which must not be deliberately planted and must be declared and disposed of at your local tip.

### Crocosmia (Montbretia)

Under the Wildlife and Countryside Act in England and Wales of 1981 it is an offence to 'plant or otherwise cause to grow these species in the wild'. Any soil containing crocosmia corms is designated as controlled waste, and needs to be disposed of at a licensed disposal site.

### Leyland cypress

Planting a Leylandii hedge and/or letting it get out of control can create legal issues. According to the Anti-Social Behaviour Act:

• A council can act against you if it deems your hedge responsible for affecting the 'reasonable enjoyment' of others.

• If part of your hedge grows over the boundary between you and your neighbour they have the right to cut it back – and the cuttings remain their property.

• You could be liable for costs or compensation if part of your hedge breaks or falls, or if it damages a neighbour's property.

• If the hedge is dangerous or obstructs a public path or pavement, your local council can take action to make you trim it back.

The Wildlife and Countryside Act of 1981 also makes it an offence to damage or destroy the nests of wild birds while in use or being built, so check before you prune or eliminate Leylandii.

# WEEDY WORDS

These are some of the most common botanical terms it is helpful to understand, explaining how weeds grow and reproduce.

**Axil** – the junction between a stem and a leaf.

**Brassica** – any member of the cabbage family (Brassicaceae).

**Bulb** – an underground storage organ in which layers of leaves and leaf bases surround a plant bud.

**Bulbil** – a small bulb, often formed above ground in an axil.

**Capsule** – a fruit that opens to release its seeds as it dries.

**Composite** – a flower consisting of many small florets, as in a daisy or dandelion. The family Compositae has been renamed the Asteraceae.

**Corm** – a swollen underground stem. Each year a new one may be created and lodge above that of the previous year.

**Crucifer** – a member of the family Brassicaceae (see above), formerly the Cruciferae.

**Dormancy** – an often essential rest period during which seeds (or other plant plants) are unable to germinate or grow.

**Hybrid** – a cross between two plants of different species.

**Node** – the part of the plant that enables leaf growth. A plant stem bears nodes at intervals.

**Pollination** – the transfer of pollen from one plant to another or, in self pollination, to the flowers of the same plant.

**Rhizome** – an underground stem that persists for more than a single growing season.

**Runner** – a creeping stem that runs above ground and from which new plants are generated at its nodes.

**Siliqua** – a long, pod-shaped fruit divided internally into two chambers. It contains a pair of valves which allow it to open and shed its seeds.

**Stolon** – an extended stem or branch that will root when it touches the ground.

**Sucker** – a new plant growing from the root of an established plant.

**Tuber** – a swollen underground stem or root from which a new plant can arise the following year. Unlike corms, tubers persist for only a single season.

**Taproot** – a long, persistent root, which may also act as an energy store for a plant.

**Umbel** – a flattened flower head consisting of many small, stalked flowers, making it look like an umbrella.

# INDEX

rhizomes 47, 52–3, 64–5, 70, 72, 74, 76, 90, 94–5, 97–9, 112–13, 120–1, 134, 135–6
Romans 13, 43, 73, 91
root nodules 87, 92
rosebay willowherb (*Chamerion angustifolium*) 80–1
Russian vine (*Fallopia baldschuanica*) 33, 97, 122–3

scarlet pimpernel (*Anagallis arvensis*) 38–9
scrofula 37, 79
seeds 11
shepherd's purse (*Capsella bursa-pastoris*) 19, 40–1
shield bugs 49
slender speedwell (*Veronica filiformis*) 47, 88–9, 136
smooth sow thistle (*Sonchus oleraceus* 42–3
soil improvers 86–7, 91, 92
spear thistle (*Cirsium vulgare*) 11, 44–5, 137
stag's horn sumach (*Rhus typhina*) 124–5
stinging nettle (*Urtica dioica*) 47, 90–1
stolons 47, 48, 80–1
stump killers 119, 123, 133–4
survival strategies 7–8
sycamore (*Acer pseudoplatanus*) 47

tap roots 21, 50, 58, 62
tools for weeding 126–7
tree seedlings 47
tubers 78–9, 82, 114–15

Virginia creeper (*Parthenocissus quinquefolia*) 123

weed soup 129
weeding 9, 126–7
weedkillers 132–6
glyphosate 31, 49, 53, 55, 57, 63, 75, 77, 85, 103, 113, 123, 134
Weeds Act 1959 137–8
white clover (*Trifolium repens*) 92–3
white deadnettle (*Lamium maculatum*) 94–5
wild violet (*Viola odorata*) 97
Wildlife and Countryside Act 1981 137–8
wisteria (*Wisteria sinensis*) 123
wood bitter-cress (*Cardamine flexuosa*) 25

yellow archangel (*Lamistrum galeobdolon*) 95